SCHAUM'S
OUTLINE OF

LATIN GRAMMAR

Alan Fishbone

SCHAUM'S OUTLINE SERIES

McGRAW-HILL
New York   Chicago   San Francisco   Lisbon
London   Madrid   Mexico City   Milan   New Delhi
San Juan   Seoul   Singapore   Sydney   Toronto

Alan Fishbone holds a Master's Degree in Classics from Columbia University. He has worked extensively as a translator of both Latin and Ancient Greek, and taught at Columbia, Colgate, and CUNY. Mr Fishbone is currently director of the Latin program at the Latin-Greek Institute in New York City.

Schaum's Outline of
LATIN GRAMMAR

10   DIG/DIG 13

ISBN 0-07-136455-2

Sponsoring Editor: Glenn Mott
Production Supervisor: Elizabeth Strange
Editing Supervisor: Ruth W. Mannino
Printed and bound by The Press of Ohio, Inc.

Library of Congress Cataloging-in-Publication Data
Fishbone, Alan.
     Schaum's outline of Latin grammar   /   Alan Fishbone.
          p.   cm.
     Includes index.
     ISBN 0-07-136455-2 (pbk.)
     1. Latin language—Grammar—Outlines, syllabi, etc.   I. Title: Outline of Latin grammar.
II. Title.

PA2100.F57 2001
478.2′421—dc21
                                                                2001030802

McGraw-Hill

A Division of The McGraw-Hill Companies

In Memoria
Mattaei Spinelli

CONTENTS

Contents

Contents

PREFACE

Schaum's Outline of Latin Grammar is a supplemental reference grammar for students who wish to review or strengthen their grasp of the fundamentals of Latin morphology and syntax. It may be used alongside any course or other material. It follows the basic structure of traditional Latin reference grammars, falling into two parts.

The first presents Latin's extensive morphology in as systematic a manner as possible, with explanations of *how* the forms of Latin words are generated. Although these forms are many and there is really no particularly easy way around memorizing them, it is hoped that the organization and regularity of their systems will speak for itself. Indeed, that organization and regularity have always been one of the fascinating beauties of Latin, despite the labor of memorization, which can sometimes obscure this from the student's view. To help students through that labor, the book contains numerous exercises, both of recognition and of form generation.

The second part deals with the basic elements of Latin syntax, increasing in complexity from noun cases to the subordination of conditional sentences in indirect statement. They are illustrated with two separate sets of exercises, the first written in a deliberately simplified vocabulary and style that seeks only to exhibit the functioning of the syntax in question. The sentences in these exercises make no other pretentions of any kind. Following them, however, are sentences drawn from classical Latin prose that also exhibit the syntax in question. These sentences are much better examples of Latin in action, but also much more difficult, and so I have included extensive vocabulary glossaries to enable students to focus on them without the tedious distraction of slogging through the dictionary. I believe that it is through these real Latin sentences that students will progress from beginning levels of competence to the ability to read classical Latin authors. In the back, students will find answers to all exercise questions and translations of all Latin.

The book is by no means exhaustive. Some things have been left out or passed over in the hope of being concise or at least not overwhelming in detail. Vocabulary, for example, has not been treated at all; likewise, some more abstruse applications of the subjunctive have been omitted. The book is, after all, an "outline." Ideally, students will be able to consult it on specific matters they encounter elsewhere, read the explanations, and practice understanding them through exercises.

I am deeply indebted to my teachers Floyd Moreland and Stephanie Russell of the Latin/Greek Institute. My thanks go to Rita Fleischer of the same for her help in the realization of this project.

ALAN FISHBONE

Introduction to the Latin Alphabet and Pronunciation

Alphabet

The Latin alphabet is the same as the English but without the letters *j* and *w*. For the most part it can be read in the same way, but a few differences must be noted.

CONSONANTS

c   is always pronounced hard, as in **cat**, never soft like an **s**.

g   is always pronounced hard, as in **god**, never soft like a **j**.

h   is always pronounced, as in **hot**, never left silent.

i   sometimes acts as a consonant before a vowel and is pronounced as the letter **y** in English.

v   is always pronounced as the letter **w** in English.

qu   is always pronounced as one consonant, sounding, as in English, like **kw**.

The other consonant letters are pronounced as in English.

VOWELS

Vowels in Latin are said to be either long or short, depending on the time taken to pronounce them within a given word.

Long vowels will be marked in this text with a horizontal bar above them. This mark is known as a *macron*.

There are differences of pronunciation between the long and short versions of the same vowels:

ā   (as in **odd**)

a   (as in **hot**)

ē   (as in **hate**)

e   (as in **pet**)

ī   (as in **feet**)

i   (as in **fin**)

ō   (as in **bone**)

o   (as in **ought**)

ū   (as in **moon**)

u   (as in **put**)

DIPTHONGS

Two vowels pronounced together as one sound make a *dipthong*.

There are six dipthongs in Latin:

ae   (as in **my**)

au   (as in **cow**)

ei   (as in **pay**)

eu   (as **read**[1])

oe   (as in **boy**)

ui   (as in **win**)

As vowel sounds, dipthongs are long.

Pronunciation of Latin Words

The accentuation of a Latin word is determined by its second-to-last or *penultimate* syllable.[2]

---

[1] This dipthong appears mostly in Greek words that have been assimilated into Latin, e.g., **Thēseus**.

[2] This rule is sometimes referred to as the law of the *penult*, this term being shorthand for the penultimate syllable of a word.

If this syllable is long, then it must be stressed, that is, it receives the accentuation when the word is pronounced. If this syllable is short, the syllable immediately before it is accentuated. (A two-syllable word will always be stressed on the first syllable.)

How is a syllable long? A syllable is long if it has a long vowel or a dipthong, or if the vowel of the syllable is followed by two or more consonants. Otherwise it is short.

īnsula	The second-to-last syllable, -sul-, is short. The vowel **u** is short, not a dipthong, and followed by only one consonant. Therefore the syllable before it, **īn-**, is accented in pronunciation.
implēvi	The second syllable -lē- is long because it contains a long vowel. Therefore it is accented in pronunciation.

Practice reading aloud the following words. Remember to consider whether the penultimate syllable is long or short.

1. mīserat
2. animālia
3. inter
4. nostrōs
5. animōs
6. urbibus
7. ambulāmus
8. salve
9. iustitia
10. sanguinis

The Noun

A noun is a word that denotes a person, place, or thing—for example, **pig**.

Every instance of a Latin noun has the three grammatical properties of number, gender, and case.

Number: Like English nouns, Latin nouns are singular or plural. This difference is shown by a change in the word's form.

e.g.,   mouse   mice   **mūs**   **mūrēs**

         pig   pigs   **porcus**   **porcī**

Gender: English nouns do not show gender. Latin has three genders—masculine, feminine, and neuter—but usually any given noun will have only one.

While nouns denoting male or female persons often show the expected gender, these genders do not necessarily correspond to the noun's meaning.

e.g.,   **fēmina,** woman, is feminine

       vir, man, is masculine

       saxum, rock, is neuter

but   **servitūs,** slavery, is feminine

       liber, book, is masculine

       forum, forum, is neuter

Case is the means by which a noun shows its meaning in a sentence. English sentences create meaning through word order. A noun shows its grammatical function by its position in the sentence or from its combination with other words such as prepositions. For example:

The pig bites the dog.

In this sentence, the pig is the subject and the dog the direct object.

The dog bites the pig.

Here the relationship has been reversed; the dog is the subject and the pig the direct object.

However, although their grammatical functions in the two sentences are different, the nouns **pig** and **dog** do not change their form to reflect such differences in meaning.

Latin nouns show these different kinds of meaning by changing their form, and the possible forms they can take are called *cases*.

Such a change in form to express meaning is called *inflection*, and Latin is an *inflected* language.

Latin has six cases. This is to say that there are six basic categories of meaning for nouns in sentences. They show these cases through their endings.

(The explanations that follow are merely a preliminary introduction. The cases will be treated more thoroughly in the sections on noun syntax.)

The Nominative Case

A noun takes the nominative case when it is the subject of a sentence:

The dog bites the pig.

If this sentence were translated into Latin, the noun **dog** would take the nominative case.

A noun also takes the nominative case when it is the *predicate* of a sentence. A predicate is a word linked to the subject in a kind of grammatical equation.

Wine is honey.

The verb acts as an equals sign, saying essentially $X = Y$, where X is the subject and Y is the predicate.

If this sentence were translated into Latin, the noun **wine** would take the nominative case because it is the subject (X), and **honey** would take the nominative because it is the predicate (Y).

The Genitive Case

This case does much the same work as the English preposition **of**.

The milk of goats is good.

Translated into Latin, the noun **goats** would take the genitive case. This case includes the meaning of the preposition **of**, so this word would not be translated.

The genitive case also shows possession. For example:

the man's house

The possessive noun **man's** in Latin would take the genitive case.

The English form **man's** itself shows inflection through the ending **'s**. You could say that the form **man's** is the genitive case of the English noun **man**.

The Dative Case

This case does much the same work as the English prepositions **to**[1] and **for**. It expresses the person(s) or, less usually, the thing(s) affected by the sentence or some part of it:

The milk of goats is good for children.

Translated into Latin, **for children** would be expressed by the word **children** in the dative case. The preposition would not be translated since the meaning **for** is included in the dative case.

The dative case expresses the indirect object of a sentence.

I gave the money to Erskine.

In Latin **Erskine** would take the dative case.

The Accusative Case

The accusative case expresses the direct object of a sentence.

The pig bites the dog.   **Porcus canem mordet.**

Since it is the direct object, the noun **dog** takes the accusative case, **canem**. **Pig** takes the nominative case, **porcus,** since it is the subject.

The dog bites the pig.   **Canis porcum mordet.**

In this sentence it is the dog which takes the nominative case, **canis,** since it is the subject, and the pig, as the direct object, which takes the accusative case, **porcum**.

This grammatical relationship is visibly expressed through case. Therefore it is not the word order that tells you the meaning of the sentence but the endings of the words.

The accusative case is also governed by certain prepositions, particularly those with a sense of (motion) toward or against.

Against the heathens.

Into the sea

In Latin, **heathens** and **sea** will take the accusative case. (See Chapter 5.)

The Ablative Case

This case does the work of the English prepositions **from/with/in/by**.

With malice

In agony

Hit by a car

---

[1] **To** in the sense of "He seems nice *to* me" but not in the sense of "Go *to* Paris."

All these nouns in Latin will take the ablative case.

This case has many uses, some of which will require prepositions and some of which will not. These will be presented more fully in Chapters 5 and 6.

The Vocative Case

This case is used only for direct address.

Son, put down that hammer.

Son would take the vocative case.

Latin also retains the vestiges of another case, the **locative**, used, as its name suggests, to express location. It is found only for nouns denoting the names of cities, towns, islands, and for the expressions "at home" and "in the country."

As stated before, these are merely introductory descriptions. Case usages will be explained in the sections dealing with noun syntax.

Exercise

1. Identify which case each noun in the following sentence would take in Latin.

   Mom, I gave the goat's milk to Douglas with my own hands.

   1. Mom   _____
   2. I   _____
   3. goat's   _____
   4. milk   _____
   5. Douglas   _____
   6. hands   _____

Declension

A declension is a system of endings used to express the different cases described above.

There are five different declensions of Latin nouns, though any given noun belongs to only one.

THE FIRST DECLENSION

Here are some sample nouns of the first declension:

puella, puellae, f.	girl
agricola, agricolae, m.	farmer
mēnsa, mēnsae, f.	table

Given above (in order) are the nominative singular, the genitive singular, the gender, and the meaning. This is the standard format found in dictionaries and textbooks.

The genitive form tells you what declension a noun belongs to and provides the stem for generating all the other case forms. As stated above, a declension is a system of endings for a noun to express case.

All first-declension nouns have the ending **-ae** in the genitive singular. The endings for the rest of the declension are as follows:

	Singular	*Plural*
Nominative	**-a**	**-āe**
Genitive	**-ae**	**-ārum**
Dative	**-ae**	**-īs**
Accusative	**-am**	**-ās**
Ablative	**-ā**	**-īs**
Vocative	**-a**	**-ae**

To decline a noun of the first declension, that is, to generate all of its possible case forms, these endings are added to the noun's *stem*. The stem is obtained by removing the ending **-ae** from the noun's genitive singular form.

For the noun **agricola, agricolae, m.**, therefore, the stem is **agricol-**. It declines as follows:

	Singular	*Translation*
Nominative/vocative[2]	**agricola**	a farmer (subject)
Genitive	**agricolae**	of a farmer, a farmer's
Dative	**agricolae**	to/for a farmer
Accusative	**agricolam**	a farmer (direct object)
Ablative	**agricolā**	from/with/in/by a farmer

	Plural	*Translation*
Nominative/vocative	**agricolae**	farmers (subject)
Genitive	**agricolārum**	of farmers, farmers'
Dative	**agricolīs**	to/for farmers
Accusative	**agricolās**	farmers (direct object)
Ablative	**agricolīs**	from/with/in/by farmers

Nouns of the first declension are predominantly feminine. The exceptions are those nouns that denote masculine agents. There are no neuter nouns in the first declension.

---

[2] With the exception of certain second-declension nouns, the nominative and vocative cases are identical and will be listed together. The locative singular for the first declension ends in **-ae**; the plural ends in **-īs**: **Rōmae,** at Rome; **Athēnīs,** at Athens.

Some more sample first-declension nouns:

aqua, aquae, f.	water
poēta, poēta, m.	poet
terra, terrae, f.	land
fīlia, fīliae, f.	daughter
lūna, lūnae, f.	moon
nauta, nautae, m.	sailor
luxuria, luxuriae, f.	luxury
fēmina, fēminae, f.	woman
amīcitia, amīcitiae, f.	friendship
pecūnia, pecūniae, f.	money
avāritia, avāritiae, f.	avarice
īnsula, īnsulae, f.	island

Exercises

2. Fully decline the noun **aqua, aquae, f.**

	Singular	*Plural*
Nominative/vocative	_____	_____
Genitive	_____	_____
Dative	_____	_____
Accusative	_____	_____
Ablative	_____	_____

3. Change the following from singular to plural. (If there are two possibilities, give both.)

1. puellam _____
2. mēnsae _____
3. poēta _____
4. terrā _____
5. aquae _____
6. fēminae _____
7. terram _____
8. pecūnia _____

4. Change the following from plural to singular. (If there are two possibilities, give both.)

1. puellae _____
2. terrās _____
3. poētīs _____
4. aquārum _____
5. mēnsīs _____
6. terrae _____
7. īnsulārum _____
8. lūnae _____

THE SECOND DECLENSION

All second-declension nouns have the ending **-ī** in the genitive singular.
   Here are some sample second-declension nouns:

ventus, ventī, m.	wind
vir, virī, m.	man
bellum, bellī, n.	war
regnum, regnī, n.	kingdom
puer, puerī, m.	boy
amīcus, amīcī, m.	friend
gladius, gladiī, m.	sword
numerus, numerī, m.	number
gaudium, gaudiī, n.	joy
liber, librī, m.	book
servus, servī, m.	slave
saxum, saxī, n.	rock

As you can see, there is considerable variety of form in the nominative singular of the second declension. It is for this reason that the genitive singular form of a noun serves both to define its declension and to provide the stem for its forms.

   The stem for all Latin nouns, regardless of declension, is obtained by removing the ending from the genitive singular form. For example:

Noun	*Stem*
ventus, ventī, m.	**vent-**
vir, virī, m.	**vir-**
bellum, bellī, n.	**bell-**
fīlius, fīliī, m.	**fīli-**

   The second declension declines as follows:

Singular

Nom.	**ventus**	**vir**	**bellum**	**fīlius**
Gen.	**ventī**	**virī**	**bellī**	**fīliī**
Dat.	**ventō**	**vīrō**	**bellō**	**fīliō**
Acc.	**ventum**	**virum**	**bellum**	**fīlium**
Abl.	**ventō**	**virō**	**bellō**	**fīliō**
Voc.	**vente**	**vir**	**bellum**	**fīlī**

Plural

Nom./voc.	**ventī**	**virī**	**bella**	**fīliī**
Gen.	**ventōrum**	**virōrum**	**bellōrum**	**fīliōrum**
Dat.	**ventīs**	**vīrīs**	**bellīs**	**fīliīs**
Acc.	**ventōs**	**virōs**	**bella**	**fīliōs**
Abl.	**ventīs**	**virīs**	**bellīs**	**fīliīs**

Note: Second-declension nouns in **-us** and **-ius** are the only Latin nouns whose vocative is different from the nominative.[3]

For all declensions, the nominative and accusative forms of neuter nouns are identical.

Nouns of the second declension are predominantly masculine and neuter.

Exercises

5. Fully decline the following nouns:

1. **saxum, saxī, n.**

	Singular	Plural
Nominative/vocative	_____	_____
Genitive	_____	_____
Dative	_____	_____
Accusative	_____	_____
Ablative	_____	_____

2. **puer, puerī, m.**

	Singular	Plural
Nominative/vocative	_____	_____
Genitive	_____	_____
Dative	_____	_____
Accusative	_____	_____
Ablative	_____	_____

3. **amīcus, amīcī, m.**

	Singular	Plural
Nominative	_____	_____
Genitive	_____	_____
Dative	_____	_____
Accusative	_____	_____
Ablative	_____	_____
Vocative	_____	_____

6. Change the following from singular to plural. (If there are two possibilities, give both.)

1. regnum   _____
2. gladiī   _____
3. virō   _____

---

[3] The locative singular ends in **-ī**, the plural in **īs**: **Tarentī**, at Tarentum; **Delphīs,** at Delphi.

4. liber _____
5. numerum _____
6. gaudium _____
7. puer _____
8. regnī _____

7. Change the following from plural to singular. (If there are two possibilities, give both.)

1. virōrum _____
2. gladiōs _____
3. bella _____
4. ventī _____
5. amīcīs _____
6. virī _____
7. numerōs _____
8. regnōrum _____

THE THIRD DECLENSION

Nouns of the third declension have the genitive singular ending **-is**.

There are two varieties of third-declension noun, i-stem and non–i-stem, with only minor differences between them. The difference amounts to the appearance of an **i** at certain points of the i-stem declension where it does not appear in the non–i-stem declension.

Here are some sample third-declension nouns:

mīles, mīlitis, m.	soldier
sīdus, sīderis, n.	star
ratiō, ratiōnis, f.	reasoning
vōx, vōcis, f.	voice, word
rēx, rēgis, m.	king
dolor, dolōris, m.	pain
nex, necis, f.	murder
flūmen, flūminis, m.	river
tempus, temporis, n.	time
corpus, corporis, n.	body
voluptās, voluptātis, f.	pleasure
amor, amōris, m.	love
eques, equitis, m.	horseman, knight

As you can see, the third declension has nouns of every gender.

There is great variety in the nominative singular, but all genitive singulars end in **-is**. The stem is obtained by removing this ending **-is** from the genitive singular form.

Noun	Stem
mīles, mīlitis, m.	mīlit-
nex, necis, f.	nec-
ratiō, ratiōnis, f.	ratiōn-
sīdus, sīderis, n.	sīder-

They decline as follows:

Singular

Nom./voc.	mīles	nex	ratiō	sīdus
Gen.	mīlitis	necis	ratiōnis	sīderis
Dat.	mīlitī	necī	ratiōnī	sīderī
Acc.	mīlitem	necem	ratiōnem	sīdus
Abl.	mīlite	nece	ratiōne	sidere

Plural

Nom./voc.	mīlitēs	necēs	ratiōnēs	sīdera
Gen.	mīlitum	necum	ratiōnum	sīderum
Dat.	mīlitibus	necibus	ratiōnibus	sīderibus
Acc.	mīlitēs	necēs	ratiōnēs	sīdera
Abl.	mīlitibus	necibus	ratiōnibus	sīderibus

i-Stem Nouns

Here are some sample i-stem nouns of the third declension:

mōns, montis, -ium, m.	mountain
urbs, urbis, -ium, f.	city
mēns, mentis, -ium, f.	mind
animal, animālis, -ium, n.	animal
nox, noctis, -ium, f.	night
nāvis, nāvis, -ium, f.	ship
mare, maris, -ium, n.	sea

i-stem nouns come formatted with an extra element, **-ium**. This is the genitive plural ending for these nouns, and it is included to indicate that such nouns are i-stem.

They decline as follows:

Singular

Nom./voc.	mōns	urbs	animal
Gen.	montis	urbis	animālis
Dat.	montī	urbī	animālī
Acc.	montem	urbem	animal
Abl.	monte	urbe	animālī

Plural

Nom./voc.	**montēs**	**urbēs**	**animālia**
Gen.	**montium**	**urbium**	**animālium**
Dat.	**montibus**	**urbibus**	**animālibus**
Acc.	**montēs, -īs**	**urbēs, -īs**	**animālia**
Abl.	**montibus**	**urbibus**	**animālibus**

Note: All i-stem nouns have **-ium** in the genitive plural.

Masculine and feminine i-stem nouns have an alternate ending **–īs** in the accusative plural. (There is no difference in meaning.) Neuter i-stem nouns have **–ī** in the ablative singular and **-ia** in the nominative and accusative plural. The locative is identical to the ablative.

Exercises

8.   Fully decline the following nouns:

   1. **corpus, corporis, n.**

	Singular	*Plural*
Nominative/vocative	_____	_____
Genitive	_____	_____
Dative	_____	_____
Accusative	_____	_____
Ablative	_____	_____

   2. **mēns, mentis, -ium, f.**

	Singular	*Plural*
Nominative/vocative	_____	_____
Genitive	_____	_____
Dative	_____	_____
Accusative	_____	_____
Ablative	_____	_____

   3. **dolor, dolōris, m.**

	Singular	*Plural*
Nominative/vocative	_____	_____
Genitive	_____	_____
Dative	_____	_____
Accusative	_____	_____
Ablative	_____	_____

9. Change the following from singular to plural. (If there are two possibilities, give both.)

    1. urbem   _____
    2. rēgī   _____
    3. vōcis   _____
    4. animālī   _____
    5. flūmen   _____
    6. urbis   _____
    7. nox   _____
    8. amōre   _____

10. Change the following from plural to singular. (If there are two possibilities, give both.)

    1. sīdera   _____
    2. voluptātibus _____
    3. urbēs   _____
    4. dolōrum   _____
    5. montīs   _____
    6. mentium   _____
    7. animālia   _____
    8. nāvium   _____
    9. amōribus   _____

THE FOURTH DECLENSION

Fourth-declension nouns have the ending **-ūs** in the genitive singular.
   Here are some sample fourth-declension nouns:

spīritus, spīritūs, m.	breath
frūctus, frūctūs, m.	enjoyment
ūsus, ūsūs, m.	use
cornū, cornūs, n.	horn
genū, genūs, n.	knee
cursus, cursūs, m.	course
manus, manūs, f.	hand
fluctus, fluctūs, m.	wave

They decline as follows:

	Singular		Plural	
Nom./voc.	**ūsus**	**cornū**	**ūsūs**	**cornua**
Gen.	**ūsūs**	**cornūs**	**ūsuum**	**cornuum**
Dat.	**ūsuī**	**cornū**	**ūsibus**	**cornibus**
Acc.	**ūsum**	**cornū**	**ūsūs**	**cornua**
Abl.	**ūsū**	**cornū**	**ūsibus**	**cornibus**

THE FIFTH DECLENSION

Fifth-declension nouns have the ending **-eī** or **-ēī** in the genitive singular, depending on whether the stem ends in a consonant or vowel.

Here are some sample fifth-declension nouns:

rēs, reī, f.   thing
diēs, diēī, m.   day
fidēs, fideī, f.   faith
speciēs, specieī, m.   appearance

They decline as follows:

	Singular		*Plural*	
Nom./Voc.	**rēs**	**diēs**	**rēs**	**diēs**
Gen.	**reī**	**diēī**	**rērum**	**diērum**
Dat.	**reī**	**diēī**	**rēbus**	**diēbus**
Acc.	**rem**	**diem**	**rēs**	**diēs**
Abl.	**re**	**diē**	**rēbus**	**diēbus**

Exercises

11. Fully decline the following nouns:

1. **fidēs, fideī, f.**

	Singular	*Plural*
Nominative/vocative	_____	_____
Genitive	_____	_____
Dative	_____	_____
Accusative	_____	_____
Ablative	_____	_____

2. **manus, manūs, f.**

	Singular	*Plural*
Nominative/vocative	_____	_____
Genitive	_____	_____
Dative	_____	_____
Accusative	_____	_____
Ablative	_____	_____

12. Change the following from singular to plural. (If there are multiple possibilities, give all.)

1. rēs   _____
2. diēī   _____
3. frūctūs _____

4. frūctuī   _____
5. genū   _____

13. Change the following from plural to singular. (If there are multiple possibilities, give all.)

1. genua   _____
2. ūsuum   _____
3. rērum   _____
4. diēbus   _____
5. rēs   _____

A Few Irregular Nouns

The noun **vīs, f.** (force, violence[4]) declines as follows:

	Singular	*Plural*
Nominative/vocative	**vīs**	**vīrēs**
Genitive	—	**vīrium**
Dative	—	**vīribus**
Accusative	**vim**	**vīrēs, -īs**
Ablative	**vī**	**vīribus**

The noun **domus, domūs or domī, f.** (house, home) declines as follows. This noun has both second- and fourth-declension forms.

	Singular	*Plural*
Nominative/vocative	**domus**	**domūs**
Genitive	**domūs/domī**	**domuum/domōrum**
Dative	**domuī/domō**	**domibus**
Accusative	**domum**	**domūs/domōs**
Ablative	**domū/domō**	**domibus**

The locative for this noun is **domī**.

The noun **deus, deī, m.** (god) declines as follows:

	Singular	*Plural*
Nominative/vocative	**deus**	**dī**
Genitive	**deī**	**deōrum/deum**
Dative	**deō**	**dīs**
Accusative	**deum**	**deōs**
Ablative	**deō**	**dīs**

---

[4] In the plural this noun means "bodily strength."

CHAPTER 1 The Noun

Exercises

14. Based on the paradigms given, identify the declension for each of the following nouns:

    1. rēgīna, rēgīnae, f.   _____
    2. speciēs, speciēī, f.   _____
    3. lītus, lītoris, n.   _____
    4. exemplar, exemplāris, -ium n.   _____
    5. currus, currūs, m.   _____
    6. ager, agrī, m.   _____
    7. saxum, saxī, n.   _____
    8. nauta, nautae, m.   _____
    9. eques, equitis, m.   _____
    10. lībertās, lībertātis, f.   _____

15. Translate the following forms according to their case and number:

    1. lībertātem   _____
    2. equitum   _____
    3. saxīs (two poss.)   _____
    4. poētae (three poss.)   _____
    5. agrōs   _____
    6. exemplar   _____
    7. lītoris   _____
    8. speciēī   _____
    9. rēgīnīs   _____
    10. speciēs lībertātis   _____
    11. rēx poētārum   _____
    12. saxa agrī   _____

16. Change the following from singular to plural. (If there are two possibilities, give both.)

    1. currum   _____
    2. exemplārī   _____
    3. rēgīnae   _____
    4. equite   _____
    5. lītus   _____

17. Change the following from plural to singular. (If there are two possibilities, give both.)

    1. poētīs   _____
    2. agrōrum   _____
    3. saxa   _____
    4. lībertātum   _____
    5. rēgīnās   _____

18. On a separate sheet of paper, decline the following nouns:

1. puella, puellae, f.
2. dolor, dolōris, m.
3. bellum, bellī, n.
4. spīritus, spīritūs, m.
5. rēs, reī, f.
6. urbs, urbis, -ium, f.

CHAPTER 2

The Adjective

An adjective is a word that modifies or describes a noun.

For an adjective to modify a noun in Latin, it must *agree* with it in gender, number, and case. Remember that gender is a permanent characteristic of a noun; only case and number are shown by ending. An adjective by itself has no gender, but reflects the gender of the noun that it modifies. Thus adjectives must be capable of showing each of the three genders.

Like nouns, adjectives belong to declensions from which they take their endings. Adjectives fall into two groups: first-second-declension adjectives and third-declension adjectives.

First-Second-Declension Adjectives

First-second-declension adjectives take their endings from the first and second declensions of nouns. That is, they take their masculine and neuter endings from the second declension and their feminine endings from the first.

Here are some examples of first-second-declension adjectives:

bonus, bona, bonum	good
malus, mala, malum	bad
dūrus, dūra, dūrum	hard
miser, misera, miserum	wretched
pulcher, pulchra, pulchrum	beautiful
dexter, dextra, dextrum	right
sinister, sinistra, sinistrum	left
frīgidus, frīgida, frīgidum	cold
magnus, magna, magnum	large, great

Given above are the nominative singular masculine, feminine, and neuter.

The stem for declining the adjective is obtained by dropping the ending **-a** from the feminine nominative singular.

As stated, these adjectives decline using the endings of the first and second declensions. They use the endings of the first declension for their feminine forms and the second declension for their masculine and neuter forms.

The stem for **malus, mala, malum** is **mal-**. It declines as follows:

	Masculine	*Feminine*	*Neuter*
		Singular	
Nominative	**malus**	**mala**	**malum**
Genitive	**malī**	**malae**	**malī**
Dative	**malō**	**malae**	**malō**
Accusative	**malum**	**malam**	**malum**
Ablative	**malō**	**malā**	**malō**
Vocative	**male**	**mala**	**malum**
		Plural	
Nominative/vocative	**malī**	**malae**	**mala**
Genitive	**malōrum**	**malārum**	**malōrum**
Dative	**malīs**	**malīs**	**malīs**
Accusative	**malōs**	**malās**	**mala**
Ablative	**malīs**	**malīs**	**malīs**

The stem for **miser, misera, miserum** is **miser-**. Such adjectives have **-er** in the masculine nominative and vocative singular. Otherwise, they decline as **malus** above.

Exercises

1. Choose the correct form of the adjective **magnus, magna, magnum** to agree with the following nouns. (If there is more than one possibility, give all.)

    1. puer   _____
    2. urbis   _____
    3. rēgīnīs   _____
    4. agricolārum   _____
    5. amōre   _____
    6. cursūs   _____
    7. rēs   _____
    8. fluctuum   _____
    9. puella   _____
    10. mentium   _____

2. Decline fully the following phrases:

1. rēx bonus

	Singular	*Plural*
Nominative/vocative	_____	_____
Genitive	_____	_____
Dative	_____	_____
Accusative	_____	_____
Ablative	_____	_____

2. urbs pulchra

	Singular	*Plural*
Nominative/vocative	_____	_____
Genitive	_____	_____
Dative	_____	_____
Accusative	_____	_____
Ablative	_____	_____

3. bellum dūrum

	Singular	*Plural*
Nominative/vocative	_____	_____
Genitive	_____	_____
Dative	_____	_____
Accusative	_____	_____
Ablative	_____	_____

Third-Declension Adjectives

Third-declension adjectives take their endings from the third declension.

Depending on the number of forms they show in the nominative singular, they are divided into adjectives of three terminations, two terminations, or one termination.

THREE-TERMINATION ADJECTIVES

ācer, ācris, ācre	sharp
celer, celeris, celere	swift

Given are the nominative singular masculine, feminine, and neuter. The stem is obtained by dropping the ending **-is** from the feminine nominative singular. They decline as follows:

	Masculine	Feminine	Neuter
	Singular		
Nom./voc.	**ācer**	**ācris**	**ācre**
Gen.	**ācris**	**ācris**	**ācris**
Dat.	**ācrī**	**ācrī**	**ācrī**
Acc.	**ācrem**	**ācrem**	**ācre**
Abl.	**ācrī**	**ācrī**	**ācrī**
	Plural		
Nom./Voc.	**ācrēs**	**ācrēs**	**ācria**
Gen.	**ācrium**	**ācrium**	**ācrium**
Dat.	**ācribus**	**ācribus**	**ācribus**
Acc.	**ācrēs, -īs**	**ācrēs, -īs**	**ācria**
Abl.	**ācribus**	**ācribus**	**ācribus**

Note: Third-declension adjectives decline like i-stem nouns, showing

-ium in the genitive plural

-ia in the nominative and accusative plural neuter

The alternate ending **-īs** in the masculine and feminine accusative plural

The ablative singular ending for all genders is **-ī**.

TWO-TERMINATION ADJECTIVES

omnis, omne	every, all
nōbilis, nōbile	noble
facilis, facile	easy
grandis, grande	big

Given are the masculine-feminine and neuter singular. This is to say that two-termination adjectives use the same form for the masculine and feminine. The stem is still obtained by removing the ending **-is** from the feminine (and, in this case, masculine) nominative singular.

They decline as follows:

	Masculine/feminine	Neuter
	Singular	
Nom./voc.	**omnis**	**omne**
Gen.	**omnis**	**omnis**
Dat.	**omnī**	**omnī**

Acc.	**omnem**	**omne**
Abl.	**omnī**	**omnī**

Plural

Nom./voc.	**omnēs**	**omnia**
Gen.	**omnium**	**omnium**
Dat.	**omnibus**	**omnibus**
Acc.	**omnēs, -īs**	**omnia**
Abl.	**omnibus**	**omnibus**

ONE-TERMINATION ADJECTIVES

simplex, simplicis	simple
audax, audācis	bold
dēmēns, dēmentis	insane

One-termination adjectives do not distinguish gender at all in the nominative singular. They do, however, distinguish the neuter from the masculine/feminine at other points in the declension.

Given are the nominative and genitive singular for all three genders. The stem is obtained by removing the ending **-is** from the genitive singular form.

They decline as follows:

	Masculine/feminine	Neuter

Singular

Nom./voc.	**audax**	**audax**
Gen.	**audācis**	**audācis**
Dat.	**audācī**	**audācī**
Acc.	**audācem**	**audax**
Abl.	**āudācī**	**audācī**

Plural

Nom./voc.	**audācēs**	**audācia**
Gen.	**audācium**	**audācium**
Dat.	**audācibus**	**audācibus**
Acc.	**audācēs, –īs**	**audācia**
Abl.	**audācibus**	**audācibus**

Exercises

3. Choose the correct form of **nōbilis, nōbile** to modify the following nouns. (If there is more than one possibility, give all.)

1. rēgī   _____
2. urbibus   _____
3. saxum   _____
4. puellārum   _____
5. amōrēs   _____
6. bella   _____
7. animālis   _____
8. speciēī   _____
9. rem   _____
10. poētās   _____

4. Fully decline the following phrases:

1. **puella dēmēns**

	Singular	*Plural*
Nominative/vocative	_____	_____
Genitive	_____	_____
Dative	_____	_____
Accusative	_____	_____
Ablative	_____	_____

2. **rēs facilis**

	Singular	*Plural*
Nominative/vocative	_____	_____
Genitive	_____	_____
Dative	_____	_____
Accusative	_____	_____
Ablative	_____	_____

5. Choose the correct forms of the adjectives **malus, -a, -um** and **grandis, -e** to agree with the following nouns:

	malus	**grandis**
1. avāritiae	_____	_____
2. fīliī	_____	_____
3. bella	_____	_____
4. animālibus	_____	_____
5. urbium	_____	_____
6. amōrēs	_____	_____
7. ventus	_____	_____
8. manūs	_____	_____
9. gaudium	_____	_____
10. rērum	_____	_____
11. nāvis	_____	_____
12. voluptātī	_____	_____
13. virōrum	_____	_____

14. montīs   _____   _____
15. tempus   _____   _____

Adjectives with the Genitive Singular in -īus

There is a group of nine adjectives belonging essentially to the first-second declension with the slight irregularity of taking **-īus** in the genitive singular and **-ī** in the dative singular. They are:

alius, alia, aliud	another
alter, altera, alterum	the other (of two)
uter, utra, utrum	which (of two)
neuter, neutra, neutrum	neither
ullus, ulla, ullum	any
nullus, nulla, nullum	no, none
sōlus, sōla, sōlum	only
tōtus, tōta, totum	whole
ūnus, ūna, ūnum	one

They decline as follows:

	Masculine	Feminine	Neuter
		Singular	
Nom./voc.	**ūnus**	**ūna**	**ūnum**
Gen.	**ūnīus**	**ūnīus**	**ūnīus**
Dat.	**ūnī**	**ūnī**	**ūnī**
Acc.	**ūnum**	**ūnam**	**ūnum**
Abl.	**ūnō**	**ūnlā**	**ūnō**

In the plural these adjectives decline as regular first-second-declension adjectives.

Note: Only **alius, alia, aliud** ends in **-ud** in the neuter nominative and accusative singular. The genitive singular for this adjective, which would have been the ungainly aliīus, is supplied by **alterīus**. All the others decline as ūnus above.

Exercise

6. Choose the correct form of the adjective **tōtus, –a, –um** to agree with the following nouns. (If there is more than one possibility, give all.)

    1. virī   _____
    2. urbe   _____
    3. mōns   _____

4. mentis   _____
5. mēnsae   _____
6. reī   _____
7. bellō   _____

Comparison of Adjectives

Adjectives are said to have three degrees:

The *positive*, e.g.,	**fat**
The *comparative*, e.g.,	**fatter**
The *superlative*, e.g.,	**fattest**

So far we have looked only at formations of the positive degree. To form the comparative and superlative degrees for any adjective, the same stem is used as is used for the positive.

THE COMPARATIVE DEGREE

The comparative degree is formed as a two-termination adjective of the third declension. For example, the comparative of **dūrus, -a, -um** (hard) is

dūrior, dūrius   harder

It declines as follows:

	Masculine/feminine	*Neuter*
	Singular	
Nom./voc.	**dūrior**	**dūrius**
Gen.	**dūriōris**	**dūriōris**
Dat.	**dūriōrī**	**dūriōrī**
Acc.	**dūriōrem**	**dūrius**
Abl.	**dūriōrī, -e**	**dūriōrī, -ē**
	Plural	
Nom./voc.	**dūriōrēs**	**dūriōra**
Gen.	**dūriōrum**	**dūriōrum**
Dat.	**dūriōribus**	**dūriōribus**
Acc.	**dūriōrēs**	**dūriōra**
Abl.	**dūriōribus**	**dūriōribus**

Note: The comparative degree declines more like a third-declension noun than adjective; all i-stem features are lacking.

The ablative singular ending may be **-ī** or **-e**.

Exercise

7.   Decline the phrase **poēta grandior**.

	Singular	*Plural*
Nominative/vocative	_____	_____
Genitive	_____	_____
Dative	_____	_____
Accusative	_____	_____
Ablative	_____	_____

THE SUPERLATIVE DEGREE

The superlative degree is formed by adding the ending **-issimus, -a, -um** to the stem. It declines as a regular first-second-declension adjective:

dūrissimus, dūrissima, dūrissimum   hardest

Adjectives ending in **-er** in the masculine nominative singular form the superlative by adding **-rimus** directly to this form:

pulcherrimus, -a, -um	most beautiful
miserrimus, -a, -um	most wretched
celerrimus, -a, -um	swiftest

There are six adjectives ending in **-lis** that form the superlative by adding **-limus, -a, -um** to the stem:

gracillimus, -a, -um   most slender

These are:

facilis, facile	easy
difficilis, difficile	difficult
similis, simile	similar
dissimilis, dissimile	dissimilar
humilis, humile	humble
gracilis, gracile	slender

Their comparatives are regular.

Exercises

8.   Decline the following phrases.

1. **rēs facillima**

	Singular	*Plural*
Nominative/vocative	_____	_____
Genitive	_____	_____
Dative	_____	_____

Accusative _____ _____
Ablative _____ _____

2. **rēgīna miserrima**

	Singular	*Plural*
Nominative/vocative	_____	_____
Genitive	_____	_____
Dative	_____	_____
Accusative	_____	_____
Ablative	_____	_____

Some adjectives do not form their comparative and superlative degrees in the regular manner.

Positive	*Comparative*	*Superlative*
bonus, -a, -um	**melior, melius**	**optimus, -a, -um**
malus, -a, -um	**peior, peius**	**pessimus, -a, -um**
magnus, -a, -um	**maior, maius**	**maximus, -a, -um**
parvus, -a, -um	**minor, minus**	**minimus, -a, -um**
multus, -a, -um	**plūs, plūris**[1]	**plūrimus, -a, -um**

9. Translate the following phrases:

1. spīritus acer _____
2. vōcēs humillimae _____
3. rēx dūrissimus _____
4. luxuria maxima _____
5. fidēs minima _____
6. mēns melior _____
7. ventus optimus _____
8. fīlius maior _____
9. gaudium dēmentius _____
10. libertās nobilissima _____
11. nāvium pulcherrimārum _____
12. animālis pessimī _____

---

[1] **Plūs** does not decline normally. It is used as a noun.

Pronouns and Adjectives

A pronoun stands in the place of a noun that is itself understood or named in the context of the pronoun's usage.

For example, normally in such sentences as "It's good" or "That's great," we know what "that" and "it" refer to. "I," "you," and so on, when used correctly, are similarly clear in their reference.

Personal Pronouns

	I	you	we	you (pl.)
Nom.	ego	tū	nōs	vōs
Gen.	meī	tuī	nostrum/nostrī[1]	vestrum/vestrī[1]
Dat.	mihi	tibi	nōbīs	vōbīs
Acc.	mē	tē	nōs	vōs
Abl.	mē	tē	nōbīs	vōbīs

There is no separate third-person personal pronoun in Latin. It is supplied by the demonstrative **is, ea, id**.

Personal pronouns in Latin function just as they do in English. However, they are not required as subjects to make an otherwise subjectless verb form complete in meaning. Their use is often emphatic.

---

[1] Of these two pairs, **nostrum** and **vestrum** are used as partitive genitives, **nostrī** and **vestrī** as objective genitives. See Noun Syntax, p. 80.

Exercise

1. Supply the correct personal pronoun as the subject of the following verb forms.

1. _____ dūcō
2. _____ ībimus
3. _____ pellitis
4. _____ clāmās

Reflexive Pronouns

A reflexive pronoun is a pronoun that refers to the subject of the sentence or clause in which it occurs. In the first and second persons, it is identical to the personal pronoun. However, there is a third-person reflexive pronoun in Latin:

Nom.	—
Gen.	**suī**
Dat.	**sibi**
Acc.	**sē**
Abl.	**sē**

This pronoun may be masculine, feminine, neuter, singular, or plural. There is no nominative because in order for the pronoun to be reflexive, it must refer to the subject. It cannot be the subject itself.

Exercise

2. Supply the correct form of the reflexive pronoun as the direct object for the following sentences:

1. _____ amāmus.
2. omnēs hominēs _____ amant.
3. _____ amātis.
4. Rēgīna bona _____ amat.

Possessive Adjectives

Related to personal and reflexive pronouns are possessive adjectives:

meus, mea, meum	my
tuus, tua, tuum	your
noster, nostra, nostrum	our
vester, vestra, vestrum	your (pl.)
suus, sua, suum	his, her, their

These conjugate as regular first-second-declension adjectives.

Personal and reflexive pronouns do not show gender in themselves, though they will in context when modified by adjectives.

There are other pronouns, however, that *do* refer specifically to nouns. Since Latin nouns show gender, number, and case, so will these pronouns. This makes them much closer to adjectives. In fact, with the exception of personal and reflexive pronouns, Latin pronouns *are* adjectives—or rather, they are words that can be either adjective or pronoun, depending on their usage.

If they *modify* nouns—that is, appear with them, agreeing in gender, number, and case—then they are adjectives. If they only refer to them, without the nouns appearing with them, they are pronouns.

In some cases, there are slight differences of declension corresponding to these differences of usage.

Demonstratives

The demonstrative pronouns/adjectives point out something:

hic, haec, hoc	this
ille, illa, illud	that
is, ea, id	this, that (unemphatic)
īdem, eadem, idem	the same
iste, ista, istud	that[2]
ipse, ipsa, ipsum	self

They decline the same way whether used as adjectives or pronouns:

	Singular			*Plural*		
	Masc.	*Fem.*	*Neuter*	*Masc.*	*Fem.*	*Neuter*
Nom.	**hic**	**haec**	**hoc**	**hī**	**hae**	**haec**
Gen.	**huius**	**huius**	**huius**	**hōrum**	**hārum**	**hōrum**
Dat.	**huic**	**huic**	**huic**	**hīs**	**hīs**	**hīs**
Acc.	**hunc**	**hanc**	**hoc**	**hōs**	**hās**	**haec**
Abl.	**hōc**	**hāc**	**hōc**	**hīs**	**hīs**	**hīs**
Nom.	**ille**	**illa**	**illud**	**illī**	**illae**	**illa**
Gen.	**illīus**	**illīus**	**illīus**	**illōrum**	**illārum**	**illōrum**
Dat.	**illī**	**illī**	**illī**	**illīs**	**illīs**	**illīs**
Acc.	**illum**	**illam**	**illud**	**illōs**	**illās**	**illa**
Abl.	**illō**	**illā**	**illō**	**illīs**	**illīs**	**illīs**
Nom.	**is**	**ea**	**id**	**eī, iī**	**eae**	**ea**
Gen.	**ēius**	**ēius**	**ēius**	**eōrum**	**eārum**	**eōrum**

---

[2] This demonstrative often implies contempt.

Dat.	eī	eī	eī	eīs, iīs	eīs, iīs	eīs, iīs
Acc.	eum	eam	id	eōs	eās	ea
Abl.	eō	eā	eō	eīs, iīs	eīs, iīs	eīs, iīs

Nom.	īdem	eadem	idem	eīdem/ īdem	eaedem	eadem
Gen.	ēiusdem	ēiusdem	ēiusdem	eōrundem	eārundem	eōrundem
Dat.	eīdem	eīdem	eīdem	eīsdem/ īsdem	eīsdem/ īsdem	eīsdem/ īsdem
Acc.	eundem	eandem	idem	eōsdem	eāsdem	eadem
Abl.	eōdem	eādem	eōdem	eīsdem/ īsdem	eīsdem/ īsdem	eīsdem/ īsdem

Nom.	iste	ista	istud	istī	istae	ista
Gen.	istīus	istīus	istīus	istōrum	istārum	istōrum
Dat.	istī	istī	istī	istīs	istīs	istīs
Acc.	istum	istam	istud	istōs	istās	ista
Abl.	istō	istā	istō	istīs	istīs	istīs

Nom.	ipse	ipsa	ipsum	ipsī	ipsae	ipsa
Gen.	ipsīus	ipsīus	ipsīus	ipsōrum	ipsārum	ipsōrum
Dat.	ipsī	ipsī	ipsī	ipsīs	ipsīs	ipsīs
Acc.	ipsum	ipsam	ipsum	ipsōs	ipsās	ipsa
Abl.	ipsō	ipsā	ipsō	ipsīs	ipsīs	ipsīs

Note: Sometimes **ipse** is called an *intensifier* because it intensifies the force of the word it modifies:

ego ipse id vīdī.   I *myself* saw it.
ego virum ipsum vīdī.   I saw the man *himself*.

Exercises

3. Supply the correct form of the demonstrative adjective in parentheses to agree with the following nouns:

1. _____ puella (hic, haec, hoc)
2. _____ montem (ille, illa, illud)
3. _____ urbium (is, ea, id)
4. _____ rēs (ipse, ipsa, ipsum)
5. _____ fīliōrum (īdem, eadem, idem)
6. _____ ventīs (hic, haec, hoc)
7. _____ rēgis (is, ea, id)
8. _____ frūctibus (ille, illa, illud)

9. _____ terrās (īdem, eadem, idem)
10. _____ vīs (ipse, ipsa, ipsum)

4.   Translate the following phrases:

1. illa rēgīna _____
2. vōs ipsī _____
3. īdem ventus _____
4. hae puellae _____
5. illa saxa _____
6. ille vīvit _____
7. ipsa venit _____
8. illa ipsa venit _____
9. fratrem ēius vīdī _____
10. ille vīvet; hic moriētur _____

Relatives

The man *who lives here* is evil.

In this sentence, the word **who** is a *relative pronoun*. That is to say, it is a pronoun which refers to a noun in the sentence and also begins a clause of its own.

In the example above, **who** refers to the noun **man**. The word to which a relative pronoun refers is called an *antecedent*.

The clause **who lives here** is called a *relative clause*. (For uses of the relative clause, see p. 119.) Relative clauses are introduced by relative pronouns.

In Latin, the relative pronoun declines as follows:

	Singular			*Plural*		
	Masc.	*Fem.*	*Neuter*	*Masc.*	*Fem.*	*Neuter*
Nom.	**quī**	**quae**	**quod**	**quī**	**quae**	**quae**
Gen.	**cuius**	**cuius**	**cuius**	**quōrum**	**quārum**	**quōrum**
Dat.	**cui**	**cui**	**cui**	**quibus**	**quibus**	**quibus**
Acc.	**quem**	**quam**	**quod**	**quōs**	**quās**	**quae**
Abl.	**quō**	**quā**	**quō**	**quibus**	**quibus**	**quibus**

Interrogatives

Interrogatives are used to ask questions. There is a slight difference in declension between the pronoun and the adjective. The interrogative adjective is identical to the relative pronoun. The interrogative pronoun joins the masculine and feminine in the singular. It declines as follows:

	Masc./Fem.	*Neut.*
Nom.	**quis**	**quid**
Gen.	**cuius**	**cuius**
Dat.	**cui**	**cui**
Acc.	**quem**	**quid**
Abl.	**quō**	**quō**

As you can see, it differs from the relative only in the nominative case and in the neuter accusative.

The plural declines in the same way as the relative.

Exercise

5. Supply the correct form of the relative/interrogative adjective to agree with the following nouns:

   1. _____ mentī
   2. _____ bellī
   3. _____ amōrēs
   4. _____ servī
   5. _____ nautae
   6. _____ fīliārum
   7. _____ montibus
   8. _____ gladiōs
   9. _____ animālium
   10. _____ rēbus

Indefinites

Indefinite pronouns/adjectives are not precise in their reference.

aliquī, alīqua, aliquod (adj.)	some
aliquis, aliquid (pro.)	someone

These decline in the same way as the interrogative, with the prefix **ali-** added.

quīdam, quaedam, quiddam/quoddam	a certain (person)
quīque, quaeque, quidque (adj.)	each
quisque, quidque (pro.)	each
quisquam, quidquam (quicquam[3]) (pro.)[4]	anyone, anything

These decline in the same way as the relative pronoun.

---

[3] Alternative spelling.
[4] The adjective corresponding to this pronoun is **ullus, -a, -um.** See p. 23.

CHAPTER 3   Pronouns and Adjectives

Exercises

6. Supply the correct form of the indefinite adjective in parentheses to agree with the following nouns:

1. _____ homō (aliquī, aliqua, aliquod)
2. _____ puerōs (quīque, quaeque, quodque)
3. _____ rēgna (quīdam, quaedam, quidam)
4. _____ flūminis (aliquī, aliqua, aliquod)
5. _____ nox (quīque, quaeque, quodque)

7. Translate the following phrases:

1. aliqua pecūnia   _____
2. quaeque rēgīna   _____
3. quoddam bellum   _____

CHAPTER 4

The Verb

Like nouns, Latin verbs are *inflected*; that is, they take different endings to express different grammatical meanings.

Their inflection is called *conjugation*. Just as nouns belong to different declensions, verbs belong to different conjugations, which are systems of endings for the expression of grammatical information. Through these endings Latin verbs show the properties of person, number, voice, mood, and tense.

Person and Number

Person and *number* refer to the subject of a verb. There are three persons and two numbers:

	Singular	*Plural*
1st	**I**	**we**
2nd	**you**	**you** (pl.)
3rd	**he, she, it**	**they**

Voice

There are two voices: active and passive. These terms refer to whether the subject performs or suffers the action represented by the verb:

Active: I bite

Passive: I am bitten

Mood

There are three moods: indicative, subjunctive, and imperative. These refer to the quality of information meant by the verb, i.e., how the listener should understand what is conveyed.

INDICATIVE

The indicative is the mood of facts. It is used for the direct assertion of facts or for questions about them:

He eats.

Does he eat?

SUBJUNCTIVE

The subjunctive is used for uncertainties, possibilities, conditions, indirect questions, and so on, both independently and in a broad range of subordinate clauses.

Its translation often involves modal auxiliaries such as *may, might, should,* and *would*;

If I *were* a rich man, I *would buy* a red car.

I was afraid he *might do* that.

In Latin the verbs italicized above would take the subjunctive.

IMPERATIVE

The imperative mood expresses commands:

Eat!

Let them eat cake!

Tense

The tense of a verb expresses the *time* and *aspect* of the action that it represents.

Time refers to whether the action takes place in the past, present, or future.

Aspect refers to whether the action is represented as *completed* or *not completed*. For example:

"He has eaten" expresses a completed action. We know from this verb's tense that the eating is finished.

"He is eating" expresses an action that is not completed.

Latin has six tenses of the indicative mood, corresponding to these three times and two aspects:

Uncompleted aspect:

(Present)	Present	I eat, I am eating
(Past)	Imperfect	I was eating, I used to eat
(Future)	Future	I will eat, I will be eating

Completed aspect:

(Present)	Perfect	I have eaten, I ate
(Past)	Pluperfect	I had eaten
(Future)	Future perfect	I will have eaten

Note: The perfect tense is capable of expressing an action in present or past time, corresponding to the English uses "I ate" and "I have eaten." In both cases, however, the action is expressed as completed.

There are four tenses of the subjunctive:

Uncompleted	*Completed*
Present	Perfect
Imperfect	Pluperfect

There are two tenses of the imperative:

Present

Future

Conjugations

Just as nouns belong to different declensions, verbs belong to different conjugations.

The process of conjugating a verb consists of adding inflectional endings to stems in different combinations to show person, number, voice, tense, and mood.

Verbs are learned according to their principal parts. These are the forms that provide the necessary stems for conjugation in all the tenses, moods, and voices. For example:

amō, amāre, amāvī, amātus	love
teneō, tenēre, tenuī, tentus	have
dīcō, dīcere, dīxī, dictus	say, tell
capiō, capere, cēpī, captus	take, capture
audiō, audīre, audīvī, audītus	hear

The first principal part is the first-person-singular present indicative active of its verb:

amō   I love

teneō   I have

The second principal part is the present infinitive active:

amāre   to love

tenēre   to have

The ending for the infinitive is **-re**. It is the vowel found before this ending that defines to which conjugation a verb belongs. There are four:

First-conjugation verbs have   **-ā-** in the second principal part: **amāre**

Second-conjugation verbs have **-ē-** in the second principal part: **tenēre**

Third-conjugation verbs have   **-e-** in the second principal part: **dīcere, capere**

Fourth-conjugation verbs have   **-ī-** in the second principal part: **audīre**

The third principal part is the first-person-singular perfect indicative active of its verb:

amāvī   I loved, I have loved

cēpī   I captured, I have captured

The fourth principal part is the perfect passive participle of its verb:[1]

amātus   (having been) loved

tentus   (having been) held

The Latin verbal system divides conjugations into two systems. The present system comprises

Present, future, and imperfect indicative

Present and imperfect subjunctive

Present and future imperatives

The perfect system comprises

Perfect, pluperfect, and future perfect indicative

Perfect and pluperfect subjunctive

Present System

All tenses of the present system are formed using the present stem. The present stem is obtained by removing the infinitive ending **-re** from the second principal part.

amā-   tenē-   dīci-   capi-   audī-

---

[1] Some grammars give the fourth principal part ending in **-tum** rather than **-tus**. However, this will serve the same purpose of providing a stem for the perfect passive system.

Note: In the third conjugation the **-e-** turns to **-i-** with the loss of the ending **-re**.

To indicate person and number, Latin employs two sets of endings, one for the active voice and one for the passive:

	Active personal endings		*Passive personal endings*	
	Singular	*Plural*	*Singular*	*Plural*
1st	**-ō, -m**	**-mus**	**-or, -r**	**-mur**
2nd	**-s**	**-tis**	**-ris/-re**	**-minī**
3rd	**-t**	**-nt**	**-tur**	**-ntur**

To conjugate the different tenses of the present system, one simply adds these endings to different versions of the present stem.

PRESENT INDICATIVE ACTIVE

For the present indicative, the endings above are added to the present stem as is. For the active voice, the active endings are used.

Sing.	1st	**amō**	**teneō**	**dīcō**	**capiō**	**audiō**
	2nd	**amās**	**tenēs**	**dīcis**	**capis**	**audīs**
	3rd	**amat**	**tenet**	**dicit**	**capit**	**audit**
Plur.	1st	**amāmus**	**tenēmus**	**dīcimus**	**capimus**	**audīmus**
	2nd	**amātis**	**tenētis**	**dīcitis**	**capitis**	**audītis**
	3rd	**amant**	**tenent**	**dicunt**	**capiunt**	**audiunt**

amant   they love, they are loving

Notes:
The present indicative active uses the ending **-ō** in the first person singular. The first person singular must be learned separately as a principal part because it cannot be derived automatically from the present stem.

The endings **-t** and **-nt** shorten preceding long vowels.

When reading a Latin verb form, analyze its components to identify it: The ending **-nt** indicates that it is third person plural active and the stem **ama-** that it is present indicative.

Some third-conjugation verbs have **-i-** in the first principal part and at other points in their conjugation. These are called i-stem verbs.

PRESENT INDICATIVE PASSIVE

For this voice the passive personal endings are used.

Sing.	1st	**amor**	**teneor**	**dīcor**	**capior**	**audior**
	2nd	**amāris**	**tenēris**	**dīceris**	**caperis**	**audīris**
		amāre	**tenēre**	**dīcere**	**capere**	**audīre**

	3rd	amātur	tenētur	dīcitur	capitur	audītur
Plur.	1st	amāmur	tenēmur	dīcimur	capimur	audīmur
	2nd	amāminī	tenēminī	dīciminī	capiminī	audīminī
	3rd	amantur	tenentur	dicuntur	capiuntur	audiuntur

Capitur   he, she, it is captured.

Notes:

The first person singular uses the ending **-or**.

The second person singular has the alternative ending **-re**. There is no difference in meaning between this and the ending **-ris**, but this form is identical in appearance to the second principal part.

The endings **-r** and **-ntur** shorten preceding long vowels.

Before the endings **-ris** and **-re**, short **-i** becomes **-e**.[2]

Exercises

1. Conjugate the following verbs in the present indicative active.

1. **dūcō, dūcere, dūxī, ductus**   to lead

	Singular	*Plural*
1st	_____	_____
2nd	_____	_____
3rd	_____	_____

2. **veniō, venīre, vēnī, ventus**   to come

	Singular	*Plural*
1st	_____	_____
2nd	_____	_____
3rd	_____	_____

3. **iaciō, iacere, iēcī, iactus**   to hurl

	Singular	*Plural*
1st	_____	_____
2nd	_____	_____
3rd	_____	_____

---

[2] This is visible in the second principal part of third-conjugation verbs. When the **-re** is removed to form the present stem, the **-e** reverts to **-i**.

2. Conjugate the following verbs in the present indicative passive.

1. **impleō, implēre, implēvī, implētus**   to fill

	Singular	*Plural*
1st	_____	_____
2nd	_____	_____
3rd	_____	_____

2. **pellō, pellere, pepulī, pulsus**   to push

	Singular	*Plural*
1st	_____	_____
2nd	_____	_____
3rd	_____	_____

3. **parō, parāre, parāvī, parātus**   to prepare

	Singular	*Plural*
1st	_____	_____
2nd	_____	_____
3rd	_____	_____

3. Identify the following forms according to person, number, and voice. Then translate.

1. implēmus _____
2. dūcitur _____
3. iaciunt _____
4. parantur _____
5. pellis _____
6. pelleris _____
7. iaciminī _____
8. parātis _____
9. dūcunt _____
10. implēmur _____

IMPERFECT INDICATIVE ACTIVE

To form this tense, **-bā-** is added to the present stem, followed by the active personal endings:

Sing.						
	1st	**amābam**	**tenēbam**	**dīcēbam**	**capiēbam**	**audiēbam**
	2nd	**amābās**	**tenēbās**	**dīcēbās**	**capiēbās**	**audiēbās**
	3rd	**amābat**	**tenēbat**	**dicēbat**	**capiēbat**	**audiēbat**

Plur.	1st	amābāmus	tenēbāmus	dīcēbāmus	capiēbāmus	audiēbāmus
	2nd	amābātis	tenēbātis	dīcēbātis	capiēbātis	audiēbātis
	3rd	amābant	tenēbant	dicēbant	capiēbant	audiēbant

dicēbās   you were saying, you used to say

Notes:

The first person singular uses the ending **-m**, which shortens preceding long vowels.

Third-conjugation verbs take long **-ē-** before the **-bā-**.

i-stem third- and all fourth-conjugation verbs show **-iē-** before **-bā**.

IMPERFECT INDICATIVE PASSIVE

To form this tense, **-bā-** is added to the present stem, followed by the passive personal endings:

Sing.	1st	amābar	tenēbar	dīcēbar	capiēbar	audiēbar
	2nd	amābāris	tenēbāris	dīcēbāris	capiēbāris	audībāris
		amābāre	tenēbāre	dicēbāre	capiēbāre	audiēbāre
	3rd	amābātur	tenēbātur	dīcēbātur	capiēbātur	audiēbātur
Plur.	1st	amābāmur	tenēbāmur	dīcēbāmur	capiēbāmur	audiēbāmur
	2nd	amābāminī	tenēbāminī	dīcēbāminī	capiēbāminī	audiēbāminī
	3rd	amābantur	tenēbantur	dicēbantur	capiēbantur	audiēbantur

amābāminī   you (pl.) were being loved, you (pl.) used to be loved

Note: The first person singular uses the ending **-r**, which shortens the preceding long vowel.

Exercises

4.   Conjugate the following verbs in the imperfect indicative active.

1. **impleō, implēre, implēvī, implētus**

	Singular	*Plural*
1st	_____	_____
2nd	_____	_____
3rd	_____	_____

2. **pellō, pellere, pepulī, pulsus**

	Singular	*Plural*
1st	_____	_____
2nd	_____	_____
3rd	_____	_____

3. **veniō, venīre, vēnī, ventus**

	Singular	*Plural*
1st	_____	_____
2nd	_____	_____
3rd	_____	_____

5.   Conjugate the following verbs in the imperfect indicative passive.

1. **dūcō, dūcere, dūxī, ductus**

	Singular	*Plural*
1st	_____	_____
2nd	_____	_____
3rd	_____	_____

2. **habeō, habēre, habuī, habitus**

	Singular	*Plural*
1st	_____	_____
2nd	_____	_____
3rd	_____	_____

6.   Identify the following forms according to person, number, and voice. Then translate.

1. pellēbāmur   _____
2. habēbāmus   _____
3. dūcēbam   _____
4. pellēbāminī   _____
5. implēbantur   _____
6. veniēbant   _____
7. habēbātur   _____
8. implēbat   _____

FUTURE INDICATIVE ACTIVE

This tense is formed differently for the different conjugations:

For the first and second conjugations **-bi-** is added to the present stem.

For non–i-stem third-conjugation verbs, the vowel of the stem changes to **-ē**.

For i-stem third- and fourth-conjugation verbs, the vowel of the stem changes to **-iē**.

Then the active personal endings are added:

Sing.	1st	**amābō**	**tenēbō**	**dīcam**	**capiam**	**audiam**
	2nd	**amābis**	**tenēbis**	**dīcēs**	**capiēs**	**audiēs**
	3rd	**amābit**	**tenēbit**	**dīcet**	**capiet**	**audiet**
Plur.	1st	**amābimus**	**tenēbimus**	**dīcēmus**	**capiēmus**	**audiēmus**
	2nd	**amābitis**	**tenēbitis**	**dīcētis**	**capiētis**	**audiētis**
	3rd	**amābunt**	**tenēbunt**	**dīcent**	**capient**	**audient**

tenēbunt they will have   **dīcēmus** we will say

Notes:
In the first and second conjugations, the first-person singular uses the ending **-ō**. The **-i-** of **-bi-** is absorbed into the **-ō**.

In the third and fourth conjugations, the first-person singular uses **-m**. The vowel **-ē-** changes to **-ā-** (short before final **-m**).

In third-person plural the **-i-** of **-bi-** changes to **-u-** before **-nt**.

FUTURE INDICATIVE PASSIVE

The same stem alterations are used with the passive personal endings:

Sing.	1st	**amābor**	**tenēbor**	**dīcar**	**capiar**	**audiar**
	2nd	**amāberis**	**tenēberis**	**dīcēris**	**capiēris**	**audiēris**
		amābere	**tenēbere**	**dicēre**	**capiēre**	**audiēre**
	3rd	**amābitur**	**tenēbitur**	**dīcētur**	**capiētur**	**audiētur**
Plur.	1st	**amābimur**	**tenēbimur**	**dīcēmur**	**capiēmur**	**audiēmur**
	2nd	**amābiminī**	**tenēbiminī**	**dīcēminī**	**capiēminī**	**audiēminī**
	3rd	**amābuntur**	**tenēbuntur**	**dicentur**	**capientur**	**audientur**

amābor I will be loved   **capiēminī** you (pl.) will be captured

Note: The **i** of **-bi-** changes to **e** before **-ris** and **-re**, and to **u** before **-ntur**.

Exercises

7. Conjugate the following verbs in the future indicative active.

1. **parō, parāre, parāvī, parātus**

	Singular	*Plural*
1st	_____	_____

2nd   _____   _____

3rd   _____   _____

2. dūcō, dūcere, dūxī, ductus

	Singular	*Plural*
1st	_____	_____
2nd	_____	_____
3rd	_____	_____

8. Conjugate the following verbs in the future indicative passive.

   1. impleō, implēre, implēvī, implētus

	Singular	*Plural*
1st	_____	_____
2nd	_____	_____
3rd	_____	_____

   2. audiō, audīre, audīvī, audītus

	Singular	*Plural*
1st	_____	_____
2nd	_____	_____
3rd	_____	_____

9. Identify the following forms according to person, number, and voice. Then translate.

   1. parābis   _____
   2. implēbō   _____
   3. dūcēmur   _____
   4. audiētur   _____
   5. pellam   _____
   6. parābuntur   _____
   7. habēbitis   _____
   8. pellēmus   _____
   9. implēbere   _____
  10. dūcēminī   _____

PRESENT SUBJUNCTIVE ACTIVE

To form the present subjunctive, the present stem for each conjugation must change its vowel.

1st	*2nd*	*3rd*	*3rd i-stem*	*4th*
amē-	**teneā-**	**dicā-**	**capiā-**	**audiā-**

Then the personal endings are added.

Sing.	1st	**amem**	**teneam**	**dīcam**	**capiam**	**audiam**
	2nd	**amēs**	**teneās**	**dīcās**	**capiās**	**audiās**
	3rd	**amet**	**teneat**	**dicat**	**capiat**	**audiat**
Plur.	1st	**amēmus**	**teneāmus**	**dīcāmus**	**capiāmus**	**audiāmus**
	2nd	**amētis**	**teneātis**	**dīcātis**	**capiātis**	**audiātis**
	3rd	**ament**	**teneant**	**dicant**	**capiant**	**audiant**

Note: The first-person singular uses the ending **-m**.

In the third and fourth conjugations, first-person singular is identical to the same form of the future indicative.

PRESENT SUBJUNCTIVE PASSIVE

The same stem alterations are used with the passive personal endings:

Sing.	1st	**amer**	**tenear**	**dīcar**	**capiar**	**audiar**
	2nd	**amēris**	**teneāris**	**dīcāris**	**capiātis**	**audiātis**
		amēre	**teneāre**	**dīcāre**	**capiāre**	**audiāre**
	3rd	**amētur**	**teneātur**	**dīcātur**	**capiātur**	**audiātur**
Plur.	1st	**amēmur**	**teneāmur**	**dīcāmur**	**capiāmur**	**audiāmur**
	2nd	**amēminī**	**teneāminī**	**dīcāminī**	**capiāminī**	**audiāminī**
	3rd	**amentur**	**teneantur**	**dīcantur**	**capiantur**	**audiantur**

The following is perhaps a helpful mnemonic device for remembering the vowel changes for the formation of the present subjunctive:

1st	*2nd*	*3rd*	*3rd i-stem*	*4th*
hĒ	wEĀrs	Ā	gIĀnt	tIĀra

Exercises

10.   Conjugate the following verbs in the present subjunctive active:

1. **parō, parāre, parāvī, parātus**

	Singular	*Plural*
1st	_____	_____
2nd	_____	_____
3rd	_____	_____

2. **faciō, facere, fēcī, factus**

	Singular	*Plural*
1st	_____	_____
2nd	_____	_____
3rd	_____	_____

11.   Conjugate the following verbs in the present subjunctive passive.

1. **habeō, habēre, habuī, habitus**

	Singular	*Plural*
1st	_____	_____
2nd	_____	_____
3rd	_____	_____

2. **dūcō, dūcere, dūxī, ductus**

	Singular	*Plural*
1st	_____	_____
2nd	_____	_____
3rd	_____	_____

IMPERFECT SUBJUNCTIVE ACTIVE

This tense is formed using the entire second principal part for its stem. The final **-e** is lengthened and the active personal endings applied:

Sing.	1st	amārem	tenērem	dīcerem	caperem	audīrem
	2nd	amārēs	tenērēs	dīcerēs	caperēs	audīrēs
	3rd	amāret	tenēret	dīceret	caperet	audīret
Plur.	1st	amārēmus	tenērēmus	dīcerēmus	caperēmus	audīrēmus
	2nd	amārētis	tenērētis	dīcerētis	caperētis	audīrētis
	3rd	amārent	tenērent	dīcerent	caperent	audīrent

IMPERFECT SUBJUNCTIVE PASSIVE

This tense is formed like the active, with the passive personal endings:

Sing.	1st	amārer	tenērer	dīcerer	caperer	audīrer
	2nd	amārēris	tenērēris	dīcerēris	caperēris	audīrēris
		amārēre	tenērēre	dīcerēre	caperēre	audīrēre
	3rd	amārētur	tenērētur	dīcerētur	caperētur	audīrētur
Plur.	1st	amārēmur	tenērēmur	dīcerēmur	caperēmur	audīrēmur
	2nd	amārēminī	tenērēminī	dīcerēminī	caperēminī	audīrēminī
	3rd	amārentur	tenērentur	dīcerentur	caperentur	audīrentur

Note: Because the entire infinitive is used as the stem, there is no real distinction among conjugations in the imperfect subjunctive.

Exercises

12. Conjugate the verb **faciō, facere, fēcī, factus** in the imperfect subjunctive active.

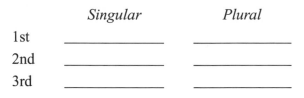

	Singular	*Plural*
1st	_____	_____
2nd	_____	_____
3rd	_____	_____

13. Conjugate the verb **dūcō, dūcere, dūxī, ductus** in the imperfect subjunctive passive.

	Singular	*Plural*
1st	_____	_____
2nd	_____	_____
3rd	_____	_____

PRESENT IMPERATIVE ACTIVE

The present imperative singular is formed by dropping the **-re** from the second principal part. The plural takes the ending **-te**:

Sing.	**amā**	**tenē**	**age**	**cape**	**audī**
Plur.	**amāte**	**tenēte**	**agite**	**capite**	**audīte**

cape!　　Take

Note:　Before the ending **-te** in the third and fourth conjugations, the stem vowel **-i-** returns.

There are four verbs that form the imperative irregularly:

Sing.		*Plur.*
dīc	say	**dīcite**
dūc	lead	**dūcite**
fac	do	**facite**
fer	carry	**ferte**

PRESENT IMPERATIVE PASSIVE

The passive imperative is identical to the second-person singular and plural of the present indicative:

Plur.	**amāre**	**tenēre**	**agere**	**capere**	**audīre**
Sing.	**amāminī**	**tenēminī**	**agiminī**	**capiminī**	**audīminī**

Note: In the singular, only the **-re** ending is used (not **-ris**). The present imperative passive is identical in form to the present infinitive active. Context will enable you to tell the difference between them.

FUTURE IMPERATIVE ACTIVE

The future imperative has both second and third persons:

Sing.	2nd	**amātō**	**tenētō**	**dīcitō**	**capitō**	**audītō**
	3rd	**amātō**	**tenētō**	**dīcitō**	**capitō**	**audītō**
Plur.	2nd	**amātōte**	**tenētōte**	**dīcitōte**	**capitōte**	**audītōte**
	3rd	**amantō**	**tenentō**	**dīcuntō**	**capiuntō**	**audiuntō**

amantō   Let them love!

The future imperative is somewhat rare, appearing mostly in legal or archaizing language.
    The future passive imperative is so rare that it will not be covered in this book.

Exercises

If necessary, refer to the following list of verbs for the exercises:

ambulō, ambulāre, ambulāvī, ambulātus	walk
clāmō, clāmāre, clāmāvī, clāmātus	shout
habeō, habēre, habuī, habitus	have
impleō, implēre, implēvī, implētus	fill
iubeō, iubēre, iussī, iussus	command
dēleō, dēlēre, dēlēvī, dēlētus	destroy
dūcō, dūcere, dūxī, ductus	lead
gerō, gerere, gessī, gestus	manage
pellō, pellere, pepulī, pulsus	push
iaciō, iacere, iēcī, iactus	throw
faciō, facere, fēcī, factus	make
veniō, venīre, vēnī, ventus	come

14. Identify the following forms according to person, number, tense, voice and mood. Do not translate. (If there is more than one possibility, give all.)

      1. ambulāmus _____

      2. ambulētis   _____

      3. ambulābat _____

      4. impleātur   _____

      5. implēbunt   _____

      6. implērēs   _____

7. pellēs   _____

   8. pellātis   _____

   9. pellitis   _____

10. dūcam   _____

11. dūcēris   _____

12. venīrēs   _____

13. dūcēre   _____

14. dūcere   _____

15. iaciāris   _____

16. iacite   _____

17. fac   _____

18. dōnābor   _____

19. dēlēbimur   _____

20. dēlēbāmur   _____

21. iubēbō   _____

22. veniāmus   _____

23. dōnāminī   _____

24. pellāminī   _____

25. dīcēbās   _____

26. habēbitis   _____

27. pellite   _____

28. iubētō   _____

29. clāmāmus   _____

30. dūcēbāmur   _____

31. iacere   _____

32. gererēre   _____

33. implē   _____

15. Translate the following forms.

   1. dīcit   _____

   2. iaciēs   _____

   3. pellunt   _____

   4. faciam   _____

   5. dēlēbantur   _____

   6. dīcimus   _____

   7. gerite   _____

   8. pellēris   _____

   9. dūcere   _____

10. veniēbātis   _____

11. ambulat   _____

12. implēbitur   _____

13. facient   _____

14. implēbāminī   _____

15. capiminī   _____

16. audī   _____

17. iubētō   _____

18. habēs   _____
19. gerētur   _____
20. ambulāmus   _____

16. Change the following forms from active to passive, retaining person, number, tense, and mood.

1. dīcit   _____
2. dūcāmus   _____
3. gerētis   _____
4. dūcite   _____
5. pellēbam   _____
6. iubēret   _____
7. dēlēbis   _____
8. cape   _____
9. iacimus   _____
10. audiam   _____

17. Change the following forms from passive to active, retaining person, number, tense, and mood.

1. iubeor   _____
2. gerēbāmur   _____
3. capiminī   _____
4. pellētur   _____
5. dēlērēre   _____
6. implēberis   _____
7. capere   _____
8. dīcuntur   _____
9. habēbāminī   _____
10. iacerēmur   _____

18. If the form is singular, change to plural; if it is plural, change to singular.

1. dēlent   _____
2. capiminī   _____
3. faciam   _____
4. gerēs   _____
5. veniēbās   _____
6. dīcar   _____
7. pellerēmus   _____
8. implēbit   _____
9. dūcētis   _____
10. habēberis   _____

Perfect System

In the perfect system, verbs of all conjugations behave the same. However, the active and passive voices are formed from different stems. Therefore, these systems will be treated separately.

PERFECT ACTIVE SYSTEM

The perfect active stem is the third principal part minus the ending **-ī**:

amāv-   tenu-   dīx-   cēp-   audīv-

All tenses of the perfect active system are formed from this stem, with no difference among the different conjugations.

Perfect Indicative Active

This tense has its own set of endings. These are added to the perfect active stem:

Sing.	1st	**-ī**	**cēpī**
	2nd	**-istī**	**cēpistī**
	3rd	**-it**	**cēpit**
Plur.	1st	**-imus**	**cēpimus**
	2nd	**-istis**	**cēpistis**
	3rd	**-ērunt**	**cēpērunt**

cepistī   you captured, you have captured

Pluperfect Indicative Active

This tense is formed by adding **-erā-** to the perfect active stem, followed by the active personal endings:

cēperam	I had loved
cēperās	you had loved
cēperat	he, she, it had loved
cēperāmus	we had loved
cēperātis	you (pl.) had loved
cēperant	they had loved

Note: The first-person singular uses the ending **-m**.

Future Perfect Indicative Active

This tense is formed by adding **-eri-** to the perfect active stem, followed by the active personal endings:

cēperō	I will have loved
cēperis	you will have loved
cēperit	he, she, it will have loved
cēperimus	we will have loved
cēperitis	you (pl.) will have loved
cēperint	they will have loved

Note: The first-person singular uses the ending **-ō**. (The **i** of **-eri** disappears before it.)

Perfect Subjunctive Active

This tense is formed by adding **-eri-** to the perfect active stem, followed by the active personal endings:

cēperim	
cēperis	
cēperit	Subjunctives should not be translated in
cēperimus	isolation.
cēperitis	
cēperint	

Note: The first-person singular uses the ending **-m**.

Apart from the first-person singular, this tense is identical to the future perfect indicative. Grammatical conditions should enable you to tell them apart.

Pluperfect Subjunctive Active

This tense is formed by adding **-issē-** to the perfect active stem, followed by the active personal endings:

cēpissem	
cēpissēs	
cēpisset	Subjunctives should not be translated in
cēpissēmus	isolation.
cēpissētis	
cēpissent	

Syncopation

Verbs whose third principal part ends in **-vī** may sometimes be shortened by eliminating **-vi** or **-ve** before endings. For example:

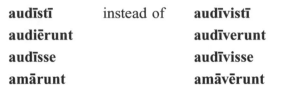

audīstī	instead of	audīvistī
audiērunt		audīverunt
audīsse		audīvisse
amārunt		amāvērunt

This phenomenon is known as *syncopation.*[3]

Exercises

19.   Identify the following forms according to person, number, tense, voice, and mood. Do not translate. (If there is more than one possibility, give all.)

1. dīxerō _____
2. amāvissēmus _____
3. dēlēverit _____
4. fēcerim _____
5. habuistī _____
6. dūxērunt _____
7. dūxerant _____
8. dūxerint _____
9. vēnistis _____
10. tenuisset _____

20.   Translate the following forms.

1. implēverātis _____
2. fēcerō _____
3. vēnistī _____
4. amāvī _____
5. iēceritis _____
6. iēcerātis _____
7. iēcistis _____
8. pepulērunt _____
9. dīxī _____
10. dīximus _____

PERFECT PASSIVE SYSTEM

The stem for the perfect passive system is the fourth principal part. It works alongside different tenses of the verb "to be,"—**sum, esse, fuī, futūrus**—to generate the tenses of this system. It is the form of **sum** that will determine tense and mood. (For the conjugation of this verb, see p. 67)

Because the fourth principal part is a participle, that is, a verbal adjective, it must agree in gender, number, and case with its subject.

---

[3] The word means a cutting or contraction.

Perfect Indicative Passive

This tense uses the present indicative of **sum** with the perfect passive participle:

ductus, -a, -um sum	I was led, I have been led
ductus, -a, -um es	you were led, you have been led
ductus, -a, -um est	he, she, it was led/has been led
ductī, -ae, -a sumus	we were led, we have been led
ductī, -ae, -a estis	you (pl.) were led, you (pl.) have been led
ductī, -ae, -a sunt	they were led, they have been led

Pluperfect Indicative Passive

This tense uses the imperfect indicative of **sum** with the perfect passive participle:

ductus, -a, -um eram	I had been led
ductus, -a, -um erās	you had been led
ductus, -a, -um erat	he, she, it had been led
ductī, -ae, -a erāmus	we had been led
ductī, -ae, -a erātis	you (pl.) had been led
ductī, -ae, -a erant	they had been led

Future Perfect Indicative Passive

This tense uses the future indicative of **sum** with the perfect passive participle:

ductus, -a, -um erō	I will have been led
ductus, -a, -um eris	you will have been led
ductus, -a, -um erit	he, she, it will have been led
ductī, -ae, -a erimus	we will have been led
ductī, -ae, -a eritis	you (pl.) will have been led
ductī, -ae, -a erunt	they will have been led

Perfect Subjunctive Passive

This tense uses the present subjunctive of **sum** with the perfect passive participle:

ductus, -a, -um sim	
ductus, -a, -um sīs	
ductus, -a, -um sit	
ductī, -ae, -a sīmus	Subjunctives should not be translated in
ductī, -ae, -a sītis	isolation.
ductī, -ae, -a sint	

Note: In the passive system the future perfect indicative and perfect subjunctive do not resemble each other.

Pluperfect Subjunctive Passive

This tense uses the imperfect subjunctive of **sum** with the perfect passive participle:

ductus, -a, -um essem
ductus, -a, -um essēs
ductus, -a, -um esset
ductī, -ae, -a essēmus
ductī, -ae, -a essētis
ductī, -ae, -a essent

Subjunctives should not be translated in
   isolation.

Exercises

21. Identify the following forms according to person, number, tense, voice,
and mood. Do not translate. (If there is more than one possibility, give
all.)

1. implētum est   _____

2. implēta erat   _____

3. implēta sunt   _____

4. pulsus sum   _____

5. iussī sumus   _____

6. audīta essēs   _____

7. dēlēta erunt   _____

8. dēlēta sint   _____

9. audītum esset   _____

10. pulsae erant   _____

22. Translate the following forms. Remember to acknowledge the gender of
the subject.

1. implētum est   _____
2. implēta erat   _____
3. iussī sumus   _____
4. dēlēta erunt   _____
5. pulsae erant   _____
6. iactum erit   _____
7. captī erant   _____
8. capta est   _____

9. amāti erunt   _____

10. amātus eram   _____

23. Change the following forms from active to passive, retaining person, number, tense, and mood. Do not translate.

    1. cēperis   _____
    2. cēperim   _____
    3. dēlēvistis   _____
    4. iēcerāmus   _____
    5. pepulisset   _____
    6. implēvit   _____
    7. implēverit   _____
    8. implēverat   _____
    9. implēvissēmus   _____
    10. dūxērunt   _____

24. Change the following forms from passive to active, retaining person, number, tense, and mood. Do not translate.

    1. ductī essētis   _____
    2. capta erat   _____
    3. captae sumus   _____
    4. captus erō   _____
    5. ductus sit   _____
    6. dēlētum erit   _____
    7. dēlētī sunt   _____
    8. dēlētae erant   _____
    9. dēlēta erunt   _____
    10. dēlētus esset   _____

25. Identify and translate the following forms.

    1. amāvērunt   _____
    2. ductī erunt   _____
    3. ambulāverit   _____
    4. iussistī   _____
    5. iussus est   _____
    6. dēlētum erat   _____
    7. dēlēverāmus   _____
    8. implēvistis   _____
    9. pepulerātis   _____
    10. cēperitis   _____
    11. ambulābās   _____
    12. pellam   _____
    13. implēbitis   _____

14. pellent   _____
15. pellēris   _____
16. pellēre   _____
17. dūciminī   _____
18. dūcēbāminī   _____
19. dūcentur   _____
20. implēmur   _____
21. implēbātur   _____
22. implēbunt   _____
23. implēbuntur   _____
24. dēlēbō   _____
25. capiēbāre   _____
26. cape   _____
27. capere   _____
28. iacit   _____
29. iacent   _____
30. iaciētur   _____
31. iactae sunt   _____
32. iēceritis   _____
33. iaciēbātur   _____
34. iactae erant   _____

26.   Identify person, number, tense, and voice for the following subjunctive forms. Do not translate.

1. cēperim   _____
2. capiāminī   _____
3. cēpissētis   _____
4. captī essētis   _____
5. caperēre   _____
6. audītum sit   _____
7. audīrent   _____
8. audiāmur   _____
9. pepuleritis   _____
10. audīvisset   _____
11. habērētur   _____
12. teneāris   _____
13. tentae sint   _____
14. tenērentur   _____
15. gerat   _____
16. ambulētis   _____
17. amārēmur   _____
18. amāvissēs   _____
19. amātus essem   _____
20. amāverim   _____

Verbal Nouns

INFINITIVES

Infinitives are so called because they lack the finite characteristics of person and number. They do, however, show tense and voice.

Present Active Infinitive

This is the second principal part:

amāre	to love
tenēre	to have
dīcere	to say
capere	to capture
audīre	to hear

Present Passive Infinitive

For the first, second, and fourth conjugations, the present passive infinitive is formed from the active infinitive by changing the final **-e** to **-ī**:

amārī	to be loved
tenērī	to be had
audīrī	to be heard

For the third conjugation, the entire **-ere** ending is changed to **-ī**:

dīcī	to be said
capī	to be captured

Perfect Active Infinitive

The perfect active infinitive is formed by adding the ending **-isse** to the perfect active stem:

amāvisse	to have loved
cēpisse	to have captured

Note: It is actually the perfect infinitive that is the stem of the pluperfect subjunctive active.

Perfect Passive Infinitive

The perfect passive infinitive is formed by adding the present infinitive of **sum** to the fourth principal part:

amātus, -a, -um esse   to have been loved
captus, -a, -um esse   to have been captured

Future Active Infinitive

The future active infinitive is formed by adding the present infinitive of **sum** to the future active participle:

amātūrus, -a, -um esse   to be about to love
captūrus, -a, -um esse   to be about to capture

Future Passive Infinitive

The future passive infinitive is formed by adding the supine to the passive infinitive of **eō**:

amātum īrī
captum īrī

This form is used very rarely. It has been omitted from the exercises.

Exercise

27.   Identify and translate the following forms.

1. habuisse   _____
2. agī   _____
3. āctus, -a, -um esse _____
4. iacere   _____
5. dēlērī   _____
6. dēlētūrus, -a, -um esse _____
7. dēlēvisse   _____

SUPINE

The supine is a verbal noun existing only in the accusative and ablative cases. It is formed as a fourth-declension noun from the fourth principal part:

Acc.	**captum**	**dictum**	**factum**
Abl.	**captū**	**dictū**	**factū**

GERUND

The gerund supplements the infinitive for complete declension of the verbal noun. It has no nominative case:

Gen.	amandī	capiendī
Dat.	amandō	capiendō
Acc.	amandum	capiendum
Abl.	amandō	capiendō

amandī   of loving

Participles

Participles are verbal adjectives. As verbs they show tense—present, perfect, and future—and voice—active and passive. As adjectives they decline and can modify nouns or act as substantives.

PRESENT ACTIVE PARTICIPLE

The present active participle is a third-declension adjective of one termination, formed from the present stem:

amāns, amantis	loving
tenēns, tenentis	having
dīcēns, dicentis	telling
capiēns, capientis	capturing
audiēns, audientis	hearing

Here is the full declension:

	Singular		Plural	
	Masc./fem.	*Neuter*	*Masc./fem.*	*Neuter*
Nom.	**dīcēns**	**dīcēns**	**dīcentēs**	**dīcentia**
Gen.	**dīcentis**		**dīcentium**	
Dat.	**dīcentī**		**dīcentibus**	
Acc.	**dīcentem**	**dīcēns**	**dīcentēs**	**dīcentia**
Abl.	**dīcentī(-e)**		**dīcentibus**	

Note: The ablative singular ending is **-ī** when the participle functions as an adjective modifying a noun. The ending is **-e** when the participle acts as a substantive or is the predicate in an ablative absolute. (See p. 94.)

There is no present passive participle or perfect active participle in Latin.

PERFECT PASSIVE PARTICIPLE

The perfect passive participle is the fourth principal part; it declines like a first-second-declension adjective.

amātus, -a, -um	(having been) loved
dictus, -a, -um	(having been) said
captus, -a, -um	(having been) captured

FUTURE ACTIVE PARTICIPLE

The future active participle is formed by adding the ending **-ūrus, -a, -um** to the stem of the fourth principal part. It declines like a first-second-declension adjective.

amātūrus, -a, -um	about to love
dictūrus, -a, -um	about to say
captūrus, -a, -um	about to capture

FUTURE PASSIVE PARTICIPLE

The future passive participle is formed by adding the ending **-ndus, -a, -um** to the present stem. It declines like a first-second-declension adjective. Its meaning contains an idea of obligation or necessity.

amandus, -a, -um	having to be loved
dīcendus, -a, -um	having to be said
capiendus, -a, -um	having to be captured

Exercise

28. Translate the following.

1. capiēns _____
2. mīles capiēns _____
3. mīles urbem capiēns _____
4. mīles urbem captūrus _____
5. captus _____
6. urbs capta _____
7. urbs ā mīlite capta _____
8. urbs ā mīlite capientī capta _____
    _____
9. urbs a mīlite aliquid dictūrō capta _____
    _____

PERIPHRASTICS

The future participle may be combined with the verb **sum** to form what are called periphrastics. They may appear in any tense.

Active Periphrastic

The active periphrastic is so called because it uses the future active participle:

captūrus sum   I am about to capture
captūrus eram   I was about to capture

Passive Periphrastic

The passive periphrastic is so called because it uses the future passive participle:

capiendus est   He must be captured
capienda erat   She had to be captured
capiendī erunt   They will have to be captured

Exercise

29.   Translate:

1. urbs dēlenda est   _____
2. urbēs dēlendae erant   _____
3. urbēs dēlendae erunt   _____
4. virī urbem dēlētūrī sunt _____
5. virī urbem dēlētūrī erant _____
6. virī urbem dēlētūrī erunt _____

Deponent Verbs

Deponent verbs are a class of verbs in Latin that, for the most part, use passive forms but have active meanings.[4]

Their principal parts are passive and three in number, functioning just as the principal parts of ordinary verbs. That is, they provide the stems for the entire conjugation of the verb.

Here are some example deponent verbs:

1st	**mīror, mīrarī, mīrātus sum**	admire
2nd	**fateor, fatērī, fassus sum**	confess
3rd	**sequor, sequī, secūtus sum**	follow
3rd i-stem	**patior, patī, passus sum**	suffer
4th	**partior, partīrī, partītus sum**	share

The first principal part is the first-person singular, present indicative passive (but active in meaning):

patior   I suffer

_____

[4] They are called *deponent* because they have "deposed" or put aside their active forms.

The second principal part is the present infinitive passive (but active in meaning):

fatērī	to confess
sequī	to follow

Note: As in the case of nondeponent verbs, the second principal part shows what conjugation a verb belongs to. Likewise the first principal part will show which verbs in the third conjugation are i-stem and which are not. For example, **sequor** and **patior** are both third conjugation. The **i** in **patior** shows that it is i-stem.

The third principal part is the first-person singular, perfect indicative passive (but active in meaning):

passus sum	I have suffered, I suffered
fassus est	he confessed
secūtī erāmus	we had followed

Deponents show all the moods and tenses of nondeponent verbs and form them regularly in the passive system. However, they do have some peculiarities.

PARTICIPLES

Though existing in the passive system, deponents do have present and future active participles that are active in both form and meaning.

Present Active

mīrāns, mīrantis	admiring
patiēns, patientis	suffering
partiēns, partientis	sharing

Future Active

mīratūrus, -a, -um	about to admire
passūrus, -a, -um	about to suffer
secūtūrus, -a, -um	about to follow

Note: This means that deponents can form future active infinitives and active periphrastics.

secūtūrus, -a, -um esse	to be about to follow
secūtūrus est	he is about to follow

Perfect

Because their passive forms are active in meaning, practically speaking, deponents have a perfect active participle:

mīrātus, -a, -um	having admired
secūtus, -a, -um	having followed
passus, -a, -um	having suffered

IMPERFECT SUBJUNCTIVE

The imperfect subjunctive, you will recall, is formed from the present active infinitive for both the active and passive.

Deponents have no present active infinitive, but they form the imperfect subjunctive as if one existed. For example, working backward from **mīrārī**, a first-conjugation passive infinitive, the active would be **mīrāre**. From **sequī**, a third-conjugation passive infinitive, it would be **sequere**. Though these forms do not actually exist independently, they act as stems for the formation of the imperfect subjunctive.

mīrārer	sequerer
mīrārēris (-re)	sequerēris (-re)
mīrārētur	sequerētur
mīrārēmur	sequerēmur
mīrārēminī	sequerēminī
mīrārentur	sequerentur

Exercises

If necessary, refer to the following list of deponents for the exercises:

cōnor, cōnārī, cōnātus sum	try, attempt
lābor, lābī, lapsus sum	slip, fall
vereor, verērī, veritus sum	fear
loquor, loquī, locūtus sum	speak
ūtor, ūtī, ūsus sum	use
morior, morī, mortuus sum	die
potior, potīrī, potītus sum	gain possession of

30. Translate the following forms.

1. lapsae erant _____
2. loquēmur _____
3. ūtere _____
4. ūtēre _____
5. moritūrus sum _____
6. verēbāminī _____
7. verēbiminī _____
8. lapsi eritis _____
9. cōnāberis _____
10. potiendum est _____
11. loquuntur _____
12. ūtitur _____

31. Identify the following forms.

1. cōnētur   _____
2. ūterēminī   _____
3. lapsī sint   _____
4. loquāmur   _____
5. moriāris   _____
6. verita essem   _____
7. ūtāmur   _____
8. ūtēmur   _____
9. ūtimur   _____
10. ūtiminī   _____

Semi-Deponent Verbs

A few verbs are deponent only in the perfect system. This is indicated by their principal parts, which are active for the present system but passive for the perfect:

audeō, audēre, ausus sum	dare
soleō, solēre, solitus sum	be accustomed to
gaudeō, gaudēre, gavīsus sum	be happy
fīdō, fīdere, fīsus sum	trust

This means that in the present they use normal active forms and in the perfect they use passive forms, both with active meanings:

loquī audeō	I dare to speak
loquī ausus sum	I dared to speak

Impersonal Verbs

There are some verbs in Latin that occur only in the third-person singular and the infinitive, without subjects. For this reason they are called *impersonal*; that is, they do not take *personal* subjects. Their principal parts reflect this, being third-person and infinitive forms:

piget, pigēre, piguit	to disgust
pudet, pudēre, puduit	to cause shame
paenitet, paenitēre, paenituit	to cause repentance
taedet, taedēre, taeduit	to weary
licet, licēre, licuit	to be permitted
oportet, oportēre, oportuit	to be proper
interest, interesse	to be of interest
rēfert, rēferre	to be of concern

For the uses of these verbs see pp. 167–168.

Some Irregular Verbs

Following are the most common irregular verbs in Latin.

sum, esse, fuī, futūrus   be

		Present indicative	*Imperfect indicative*	*Future indicative*	*Present subjunctive*
Sing.	1st	sum	eram	erō	sim
	2nd	es	erās	eris	sīs
	3rd	est	erat	erit	sit
Plur.	1st	sumus	erāmus	erimus	sīmus
	2nd	estis	erātis	eritis	sītis
	3rd	sunt	erant	erunt	sint

Note: The fourth principal part is the future active participle. This verb does not (and could not) have a passive system.

Sum has no present or perfect participles. It is regular in the imperfect subjunctive and the entire perfect system.

The future infinitive of **sum** is **futūrum esse**. However, in addition to this form there is the alternate **fore**. This form is also often used as the stem for the imperfect subjunctive, particularly for the third-person singular form **foret**.

possum, posse, potuī, ...   **be able**

		Present indicative	*Imperfect indicative*	*Future indicative*	*Present subjunctive*
Sing.	1st	possum	poteram	poterō	possim
	2nd	potes	poterās	poteris	possīs
	3rd	potest	poterat	poterit	possit
Plur.	1st	possumus	poterāmus	poterimus	possīmus
	2nd	potestis	poterātis	poteritis	possītis
	3rd	possunt	poterant	poterunt	possint

This verb is compounded from **sum**. Before forms of **sum** beginning with the letter **s**, it prefixes **pos-**. Before forms beginning with the letter **e**, it prefixes **pot-**.

It forms the perfect regularly from its own stem **potu-**.

eō, īre, iī/īvī, itus   to go

		Present indicative	*Imperfect indicative*	*Future indicative*	*Present subjunctive*
Sing.	1st	eō	ībam	ībō	eam
	2nd	īs	ībās	ībis	eās
	3rd	it	ībat	ībit	eat

Plur.	1st	īmus	ībāmus	ībimus	eāmus
	2nd	ītis	ībātis	ībitis	eātis
	3rd	eunt	ībant	ībunt	eant

PRESENT PARTICIPLE

iēns, euntis

The rest of its conjugation is regular.

volō, velle, voluī	wish, be willing
nōlō, nōlle, nōluī	be unwilling
mālō, mālle, māluī	want more, prefer

PRESENT INDICATIVE

Sing.	1st	volō	nōlō	mālō
	2nd	vīs	nōn vīs	māvīs
	3rd	vult	nōn vult	māvult
Plur.	1st	volumus	nōlumus	mālumus
	2nd	vultis	nōn vultis	māvultis
	3rd	volunt	nōlunt	mālunt

IMPERFECT INDICATIVE

Sing.	1st	volēbam	nōlēbam	mālēbam
	2nd	volēbās	nōlēbās	mālēbās
	3rd	volēbat	nōlēbat	mālēbat
Plur.	1st	volēbāmus	nōlēbāmus	mālēbāmus
	2nd	volēbātis	nōlēbātis	mālēbātis
	3rd	volēbant	nōlēbant	mālēbant

FUTURE INDICATIVE

Sing.	1st	volam	nōlam	mālam
	2nd	volēs	nōlēs	mālēs
	3rd	volet	nōlet	mālet
Plur.	1st			
	2nd	etc. (as regular third conjugation)		
	3rd			

PRESENT SUBJUNCTIVE

Sing.	1st	**velim**	**nōlim**	**mālim**
	2nd	**velīs**	**nōlīs**	**mālīs**
	3rd	**velit**	**nōlit**	**mālit**
Plur.	1st	**velīmus**	**nōlīmus**	**mālīmus**
	2nd	**velītis**	**nōlītis**	**mālītis**
	3rd	**velint**	**nōlint**	**mālint**

PRESENT PARTICIPLE

volēns, volentis   nōlēns, nōlentis

mālō has no present participle
   These verbs are regular in the imperfect subjunctive and the perfect system.

ferō, ferre, tulī, latus   bear, carry

PRESENT INDICATIVE

		Active	*Passive*
Sing.	1st	**ferō**	**feror**
	2nd	**fers**	**ferris, ferre**
	3rd	**fert**	**fertur**
Plur.	1st	**ferimus**	**ferimur**
	2nd	**fertis**	**feriminī**
	3rd	**ferunt**	**feruntur**

IMPERATIVE

Sing.	**fer**
Pl.	**ferte**

Otherwise, ferō acts as a regular third conjugation verb.

fīō, fierī, factus sum   be done, be made, happen

This verb is used as the passive for the present system of the verb.

   faciō, facere, fēcī, factus

It has active forms with passive meanings and conjugates as a regular i-stem third-conjugation verb. Note that it has a long -ī- in the stem:

		Present indicative	*Imperfect indicative*	*Future indicative*	*Present subjunctive*
Sing.	1st	**fīō**	**fīēbam**	**fīam**	**fīam**
	2nd	**fīs**	**fīēbās**	**fīēs**	**fīās**
	3rd	**fit**	**fīēbat**	**fīet**	**fīat**
Plur.	1st	**fīmus**	**fīēbāmus**	**fīēmus**	**fīāmus**
	2nd	**fītis**	**fīēbātis**	**fīētis**	**fīātis**
	3rd	**fīunt**	**fīēbant**	**fīent**	**fīant**

ōdī, ōdisse   hate

As the principal parts indicate, this verb exists only in the perfect tense. However in the perfect it has present meaning.

ōdistī   you hate

Its pluperfect tense acts as a simple past and its future perfect as a simple future:

ōderam   I hated
ōderit   he will hate

Because this verb lacks a present system, it is called a *defective* verb.

Exercise

32.   Translate the following forms:
1. erimus   _____
2. nōlunt   _____
3. poteritis   _____
4. possunt   _____
5. vultis   _____
6. ībit   _____
7. fers   _____
8. fīmus   _____
9. ferris   _____
10. māvultis   _____
11. nōlumus   _____
12. ībam   _____
13. poterās   _____
14. estis   _____
15. nōlle   _____
16. fierī   _____
17. feriminī   _____
18. īs   _____
19. volam   _____

CHAPTER 4 The Verb

20. mālunt   _____
21. nōluit   _____
22. ferre   _____
23. iēns   _____
24. potestis   _____
25. posse   _____

CHAPTER 5

Adverbs and Prepositions

Adverbs

Adverbs are words that modify verbs, adjectives, or other adverbs. They answer questions such as How? Where? When?

He wept **bitterly**.

The adverb **bitterly** modifies the verb **wept** and tells us *how* he wept.

I am **extremely** fat.

The adverb **extremely** modifies the adjective **fat** and tells us *how* fat I am.

Adverbs are formed from adjectives in one of two different ways. First-second-declension adjectives form adverbs by adding the ending **-ē** to the stem:

amīcē	in a friendly manner
miserē	wretchedly

Third-declension adjectives form adverbs by adding the ending **-iter** to the stem:

fortiter	bravely
ācriter	sharply

Sometimes the neuter accusative singular of an adjective will serve as an adverb:

multum	much
facile	easily

The comparative degree of the adverb is supplied by the neuter accusative singular of the comparative adjective:

ācriter	sharply	**ācrius**	more sharply
miserē	wretchedly	**miserius**	more wretchedly

The superlative degree of the adverb is formed as the adverb of a regular first-second-declension adjective, with the ending **-ē**

fortissimē	most bravely
ācerrimē	most sharply

Some common adverbs are irregular in all degrees:

bene	well	**melius**	better	**optimē**	best
male	badly	**peius**	worse	**pessimē**	worst
parum	too little	**minus**	less	**minimē**	least
multum	much	**plūs**	more	**maximē**	most greatly

Exercise

1. Generate the appropriate adverb in the positive, comparative, and superlative degrees for the following adjectives:

	Positive	*Comparative*	*Superlative*
1. nōbilis	_____	_____	_____
2. acerbus	_____	_____	_____
3. miser	_____	_____	_____
4. malus	_____	_____	_____
5. bonus	_____	_____	_____

Prepositions

Prepositions are words placed before nouns to create phrases that express adverbial meanings. They answer questions such as Where? Why? How? When?

The pig slept **under the table**.

The preposition **under** combines with the noun **table** to tell us *where* the pig slept.
    Prepositions in Latin take the accusative or the ablative case. Some may take both.

COMMON PREPOSITIONS WITH THE ACCUSATIVE CASE

ad	to, toward	They set out toward Asia
	ad Asiam proficiscuntur	
	for,[1] with a view to	
	ad pacem	for peace
ante	before (in space or time)	
	ante oppidum	before the town
	ante bellum	before the war
apud	at, near	
	apud Rhēnum	at the Rhine
	at the house of	
	cēnābis bene *apud mē*	you will dine well *at my house*
circum	around	
	circum castra	around the camp
contrā	against	
	contrā illum dīcō	I speak against that man
inter	among	
	inter mortuōs	among the dead
	between	
	inter meam opīniōnem ac tuam	between my opinion and yours
ob	on account of, because of	
	ob metum	because of fear
per	through (in different senses)	
	multa per aequora vectus	conveyed through many seas
	nihil per īram actum est	nothing was done through anger
post	behind	
	post montem	behind the mountain
	after	
	post mortem	after death
praeter	beyond	
	praeter īnsulās	beyond the islands
	praeter spem	beyond expectation
propter	on account of	
	propter amōrem	on account of love
trans	across	
	trans flūmen	across the river

---

[1] "For" in the sense of purpose (i.e., "I did it 'for money'", not in the sense of "a gift 'for you.'"

COMMON PREPOSITIONS WITH THE ABLATIVE CASE

ā, ab[2]	away from	
	ā Britanniā	away from Britain
	by[3]	
	interfectus est ā Caesare	he was killed by Caesar
cum	with	
	cum amīcīs	with friends
	Personal, relative, and interrogative pronouns attach to the end of this word:	
	mēcum	with me
	quibuscum?	with whom?
dē	down from	
	dē montibus	down from the mountains
	concerning	
	dē animā	concerning the soul
ē, ex[4]	out of	
	ē prōvinciā īre	to go out of the province
prō	for, on behalf of	
	prō amīcō meō	on behalf of my friend
sine	without	
	sine pugnā et sine vulnere	without a fight and without injury

PREPOSITIONS THAT TAKE BOTH ACCUSATIVE AND ABLATIVE CASES

in	+acc	
	into	
	in Asiam ībit	he will go into Asia
	against	
	ōrātiō in Catilīnam	a speech against Catiline
	+abl	
	in, on	
	in Asiā est	he is in Asia
	in tantā maestitiā fuisse	to have been in such great sadness

---

[2] Generally, the form **ab** is used before a word beginning with a vowel, and **ā** before a word beginning with a consonant.

[3] In the sense of an action performed "by" a person. This kind of prepositional phrase usually occurs with verbs in the passive voice and constitutes the ablative of personal agent. See p. 92.

[4] Generally the form **ex** is used before a word beginning with a vowel, and **ē** before a word beginning with a consonant.

sub   +acc
>   under (implying motion)
>   **sub portam venient**   they will come beneath the gate

+abl
>   under (stationary)
>   **quidquid sub terrā est**   whatever is beneath the earth

Exercise

2.   Translate the following phrases:

1. sub lūnā   _____
2. post bellum   _____
3. apud rēgem   _____
4. circum urbem   _____
5. per agrōs   _____
6. sine amōre   _____
7. ex aquā   _____
8. cum avāritiā   _____
9. dē montibus   _____
10. contrā mīlitēs   _____
11. ob pecūniam   _____
12. prō rēgīnā   _____
13. trans mare   _____
14. ante diem   _____
15. ā poētā   _____

CHAPTER 6

Syntax of the Noun

Nominative Case

SUBJECT

The nominative case is the case for the subject of a sentence:

Poēta vincit. The poet conquers.

Poēta is in the nominative case because it is the subject of this sentence.

Any adjective used to modify this subject must agree with it in gender and number, as well as case.

Poēta miser vincit. The wretched poet conquers.

Miser is masculine nominative singular to agree with **poēta**.

PREDICATE NOMINATIVE

The nominative case is also used in the following manner:

Poēta est miser. The poet is wretched.

or

Poēta est servus. The poet is a slave.

In these sentences **poēta** is still the subject. The function of the sentence is to make a statement about this subject, saying essentially "$X = Y$," with the verb acting as an equal sign.

Poēta	est	miser
X	$=$	Y

This *Y* is called a *predicate*, and it agrees in case with the subject. Therefore, in the sentences on page 79, **miser** and **servus** are called *predicate nominatives*.

Genitive Case

The genitive case has many meanings in common with the English preposition **of**. For example:

poēta *amōris*.   a poet *of love.*
amor *pecūniae*.   love *of money.*

A noun in the genitive case usually follows another noun and gives information about it. Above, **amōris** tells us something about what kind of poet she is, **pecūniae** about what kind of love it is. In other words, the genitive case functions like an adjective.

POSSESSIVE GENITIVE

terra *rēgis*   the land *of the king*

This genitive shows possession or ownership.

PARTITIVE GENITIVE

numerus *virōrum*   a number *of men*
lībra *aurī*   a pound *of gold*

The partitive genitive expresses the whole from which a *part* has come. This genitive is often found with superlatives:

Ille vir est optimus *poētarum*   That man is the best *of the poets*

OBJECTIVE GENITIVE

amor *pecūniae*   love *of money*
nex *animālium*   slaughter *of animals*

The objective genitive follows a noun that has a verbal idea in its meaning.

amor	**amō, amāre**	to love
nex	**necō, necāre**	to kill

The use of genitive then corresponds to the *direct object* of the verbal idea contained in that noun:

to love money

In the phrase **amor pecūniae**, the genitive "of money" represents the direct object of the verbal idea of "love." Therefore, it is called an *objective* genitive.

SUBJECTIVE GENITIVE

amor *mātris*	the love *of a mother*
adventus *nāvis*	the arrival *of the ship*

Like the objective genitive, the subjective genitive follows a noun with a verbal idea in its meaning, e.g., "to love," "to arrive." This genitive corresponds to the *subject* of that verbal idea:

> The mother loves.
>
> The ship arrives.

Therefore, it is called a *subjective* genitive.

GENITIVE OF CHARACTERISTIC, OR PREDICATE GENITIVE

Hominum **est pecūniam amāre**   It is *characteristic of men* to love money

This genitive is almost always used in sentences of this kind, often with an infinitive as the subject, saying that a certain type of action is "characteristic of" someone or something. Such a sentence has the form $X = Y$, i.e.,

Pecūniam amāre	**est**	**hominum**
X	$=$	Y

The genitive functions as the predicate, and so this type of construction is also called a *predicate* genitive.

GENITIVE OF DESCRIPTION

vir *magnae avāritiae*   a man *of great avarice*

This genitive together with an adjective makes a phrase that *describes* another noun.

GENITIVE OF INDEFINITE VALUE

Illud cōnsilium *magnī* **aestimō.**   **I reckon that advice** *of great (value).*

As the name suggests, this genitive is used to make an unspecified judgment of value.

GENITIVE WITH CERTAIN VERBS

Certain verbs, such as some impersonal verbs (see p. 167) and those denoting remembering or forgetting, take the genitive case.

Pecūniae **taedet poētam.**   The poet feels disgust *of money.*
Oblīviscāminī *bellōrum.*   Let us be forgetful *of wars.*

These should be learned as a matter of vocabulary with such verbs.

Exercises

1. Translate the following. Then identify the case and usage of the italicized word(s).

  1. Puer est *fīlius* nautae.

  2. Avāritia est amor *pecūniae.*
  _____

  3. Gaudium amīcōrum est *magnum.*
  _____

  4. Gaudium magnum *amīcōrum* audiō.
  _____

  5. gladius *fīliae*
  _____

  6. spīritus *deī*
  _____

  7. dolor *servōrum* caecōrum
  _____

  8. *Fīliōrum* est patrēs amāre.
  _____

  9. animal *cornuum magnōrum*
  _____

  10. cornua *animālium*
  _____

  11. Illam rēgīnam *nihilī* aestimō.
  _____

2. Translate the following sentences.

  1. Ut igitur in sēminibus est causa arbōrum et stirpium, sīc huius luctuōsissimī bellī tū sēmen fuistī.
  _____
  _____
  _____
  _____

2. Ut Helena Trōiānīs sic iste huic reī pūblicae bellī causa, causa pestis atque exitī fuit.

_____

_____

_____

3. Et nōmen pācis dulce est et ipsa rēs salūtāris; sed inter pācem et servitūtem plūrimum interest. Pax est tranquilla lībertās, servitūs postrēmum malōrum omnium, nōn modo bellō sed morte etiam repellendum.

_____

_____

_____

_____

4. Maximus vīnī numerus fuit, permagnum optimī pondus argentī... Hōrum paucīs diēbus nihil erat.

_____

_____

5. Nōn minus est imperātōris cōnsiliō superāre quam gladiō.

_____

6. Iūcundiōrem faciet lībertātem servitūtis recordātiō.

_____

7. Nōn putat tua dōna esse tantī.

_____

_____

Vocabulary

ut	just as
igitur (adv.)	therefore
sēmen, sēminis, n.	seed
arbor, -ōris, m.	tree
stirps, stirpis, -ium, f.	plant
sīc	so
luctuōsus, -a, -um	distressing, grievous
Helena, -ae, f.	Helen
Trōiānus, -a, -um	Trojan
pestis, pestis, f.	destruction, pestilence
nōmen, nōminis, n.	name

pax, pācis, f.	peace
dulcis, -e	sweet
salūtāris, -e	beneficial, healthful
servitūs, -tūtis, f.	slavery
tranquillus, -a, -um	peaceful, tranquil
lībertās, -tātis, f.	freedom
postrēmus, -a, -um	most extreme
nōn modo	not only
sed etiam	but also
mors, mortis, f.	death
repellō, repellere	repel
numerus, -ī, m.	number, amount
vīnum, -ī, n.	wine
pondus, ponderis, n.	weight, quantity
argentum, -ī, n.	silver
paucī, -ae, -a	few
imperātor, -ōris, m.	commander
cōnsilium, -ī, n.	advice, planning
gladius, -ī, m.	sword
iūcundus, -a, -um	pleasing
recordātiō, -ōnis, f.	recollection, memory
lībertās, -tātis, f.	liberty
servitūs, -tūtis, f.	slavery
putō, putāre	think
tantus, -a, -um	so great

Dative Case

The dative case can often be translated by the English prepositions **to** and **for**.

Aqua est bona *puerīs*.   Water is good *for children*.

Almost always you will find nouns that denote people in the dative case; these are the people "to" or "for" whom the information in the rest of the sentence is important.

INDIRECT OBJECT

The dative is used to express the indirect object of a sentence.

Librum *poētae* **dedī.**   I gave a book *to the poet*.
Pecūniam *tibi* **mōnstrābō.**   I will show the money *to you*.

DATIVE OF THE POSSESSOR

This dative is used in a complete sentence to say that something belongs "to someone."

Rēgī **sunt multa animālia.**   *To the king* there are many animals.
                                       or
                                       The king has many animals.

PREDICATE DATIVE

This is an old and interesting use of the dative that does not much resemble its other uses.

  Illa terra erit *magno ūsuī*.

Some suggested translations have been:

  That land will be "of great use."

              "a source of great use."

              "for the purpose of great use."

The sentence has the form of an equation in which the dative acts as the predicate:

  Illa terra   **erit**   **magnō usuī**
      X   =   *Y*

Ventus est magnae cūrae.   The wind is a great concern.

This usage is often accompanied by another, more ordinary dative of reference to specify for whom the sentence is true:

Nautīs **ventus est magnae cūrae.**   *To the sailors* the wind is a (source of)
                                          great concern.

DATIVE WITH COMPOUND VERBS

Many compound verbs, that is, verbs with prepositional prefixes attached to them, call for a referential dative:

Rōmānī servitūtem *populīs*
  imposuērunt.   The Romans imposed slavery *on the
                                         peoples*.

It is as if the prefix is a preposition pointing to the dative.

Mūrum urbī circumposuit.   He put a wall around the city.

DATIVE WITH CERTAIN INTRANSITIVE VERBS

Certain intransitive verbs, that is, verbs that do not take direct objects, naturally take the dative case:

Poētīs persuādēmus abīre.   We persuade *the poets* to go away.
Rēgī nōn crēdō.   I do not trust the king.

This dative should be learned as a matter of vocabulary with the verbs that take it.

DATIVE OF AGENT

This dative is used mostly with the passive periphrastic (see p. 63)

Urbs vincenda est *mīlitibus*.   The city must be conquered *by the soldiers.*

(Literally, "For the soldiers it is necessary for the city to be conquered.")

Exercises

3.   Translate the following. Then identify the italicized usages.

1. *Mihi* nōn est gladius.

_____

_____

_____

2. Rēx pecūniam *mīlitibus* dōnābat.

_____

_____

_____

3. Nāvis *poētis* dēlenda erat.

_____

_____

_____

4. Urbs *magnae luxūriae* nautīs dēlenda erat.

_____

_____

_____

5. Illa aqua *puerīs* nocēbit.

_____

_____

_____

6. Undae *magnō perīculō* nāvibus sunt.

_____

_____

_____

7. Exercitum *montibus* postposuit.

_____

_____

_____

4. Translate the following sentences.

1. Parant ea quae ūsuī sunt oppidō.

_____

2. Ille Rōmānae praeerat arcī.

_____

3. Quam attulistī ratiōnem populō Rōmānō?

_____

4. Aliīs cōnsilium, aliīs animus, aliīs occāsiō dēfuit; voluntās nēminī.

_____

_____

5. Mortem servitūtī antepōnāmus.

_____

_____

Vocabulary

parō, parāre, parāvī, parātus	prepare
ūsus, -ūs, m.	use, advantage
praesum	to be in charge of
arx, arcis, f.	citadel
afferō	bring to
ratiō, -ōnis, f.	reason, reckoning
cōnsilium, -ī, n.	advice, planning
occāsiō, -ōnis, f.	opportunity
dēsum	to be lacking to (+ dative)
voluntās, -tātis, f.	will, intention
nēmō, nēminis	nobody
mors, mortis, f.	death
servitūs, -tūtis, f.	slavery
antepōnō	place before, prefer

Accusative Case

DIRECT OBJECT

The accusative is used to express the direct object of a sentence.

Mīlitēs *urbem* dēlent. The soldiers destroy *the city.*

    Sometimes a verb that would not normally take a direct object, e.g., **eō**, *to go*, can take one naturally connected to its meaning.

iter **īre** to go a road
viam **cēdere** to go a road

Such a usage is called an *internal* or *cognate* accusative.

SUBJECT ACCUSATIVE OF AN INFINITIVE

Infinitives take subjects in the accusative case, most commonly in what is called indirect statement, that is, speech reported from another source. The grammar of this construction is explained in Chapter 8.

Dīcō *virōs* in via ambulāre. I say that *the men* are walking in the road.

ACCUSATIVE OF EXTENT OF TIME OR SPACE

This is an adverbial usage, limiting the time or space occupied by an action.

Quīnque annōs **labōrāveram.** I had worked *for five years.*
Sex mīlia **passuum processērunt.** They advanced *six miles.*

ADVERBIAL ACCUSATIVE

The neuter singular accusative of an adjective can function as an adverb.

Multum **pecūniam amātis.** You love money very much.

ACCUSATIVE OF PLACE TO WHICH

The accusative, with or without prepositions, is used to express motion toward or against something.

Ad mare vēnimus. We came *to the sea.*
in mīlitēs against the soldiers

Prepositions are not used for the names of cities, towns, or islands, or the nouns **domus** and **rūs**.

Rōmam ībō.   I will go *to Rome.*
Domum vēnimus.   We came *home.*

ACCUSATIVE WITH PREPOSITIONS

Many other ideas are expressed by the accusative with different prepositions (see p. 75).

ACCUSATIVE OF EXCLAMATION

The accusative is used for exclamations:

O rem terribilem!   A terrible thing!

Exercises

5. Translate the following. Then identify the italicized usages.

1. Pecūnia *amīcitiam* dēlēbit.

2. *Tōtam noctem* ambulāvī.

3. *Viam* difficilem nōlumus īre.

4. *Rōmam* fēminae processērunt.

5. Dīcō *pecūniam* amīcitiam dēlēre.

6. Dīcit *virōs* clāmāre.

7. Avāritia *mentem* rēgis dēlēvit.

8. Multōs *annōs* avāritia mentem rēgis dēlēbat.

_____

_____

_____

6. Translate the following sentences.

1. Habet quidem certē rēs pūblica adulescentīs nōbillissimōs parātōs dēfensōrēs.

_____

_____

2. Hanc vērō taeterrimam bēluam quis ferre potest aut quō modō? Quid est in Antōniō praeter libīdinem, crūdēlitātem, petulantiam, audāciam?

_____

_____

_____

3. Pōne ante oculōs laetitiam senātūs populīque Rōmānī.

_____

_____

4. Bellum nefārium contrā ārās et focōs, contrā vītam fortūnāsque nostrās ab homine prōflīgātō ac perditō nōn comparārī sed gerī iam vīderam.

_____

_____

_____

_____

5. At quam multōs diēs in eā villā turpissimē es perbacchātus!

_____

_____

6. O foedītātem hominis flāgitiōsam, o impudentiam, nēquitiam, libīdinem nōn ferandam!

_____

_____

_____

Vocabulary

quidem (adv.)	indeed
certē (adv.)	certainly
adulescēns, -ntis	young, youthful
parō, parāre	prepare
dēfensor, -ōris, m.	defender
vērō	but

taeter, -tra, -trum	foul
bēlua, -ae, f.	beast
quō modō	how?
Antōnius, -ī, m.	Antonius
libīdō, -inis, f.	lust
crūdēlitās, -tātis, f.	cruelty
petulantia, -ae, f.	arrogance
audācia, -ae, f.	outrageous boldness, audacity
laetitia, -ae, f.	happiness
senātus, -us, m.	senate
nefārius, -a, -um	evil, unspeakably criminal
āra, -ae, f.	altar
focus, -ī, m.	hearth, fireplace
prōflīgātus, -a, -um	profligate
perditus, -a, -um	ruined, desperate
comparō, comparāre	prepare, get ready
at	but
villa, -ae, f.	villa
turpis, -e	foul
perbacchor (1st conjug.)	revel, have wild parties
foeditās, -tātis, f.	repulsiveness, baseness
flāgitiōsus, -a, -um	disgraceful
impudentia, -ae, f.	shamelessness
nēquitia, -ae, f.	worthlessness

Ablative Case

The ablative does many of the jobs of the English prepositions **from**, **with**, **in**, and **by**. They are many.

ABLATIVE OF PLACE FROM WHICH (FROM)

Prepositions denoting ideas of separation take the ablative case:

ex urbe	out of the city
dē montibus	down from the mountains
ab aquā	away from the water

Names of cities, towns, and islands and the nouns **domus** and **rūs** do not take prepositions to express this meaning.

| *Rōmā* vēnērunt. | They came *from Rome*. |
| *Rūre* vēnērunt. | They came *from the country*. |

ABLATIVE OF PLACE WHERE (IN)

This ablative takes the preposition **in**.

| **in Asiā** | in Asia |
| **in terrīs** | in the lands |

Names of cities, towns, and islands and the nouns **domus** and **rūs** do not take the preposition **in** to express this meaning. They take the locative case (see p. 97).

ABLATIVE OF TIME WHEN OR WITHIN WHICH (IN)

These ablatives situate an event in time.

illō diē	on that day
eō tempore	at that time
Quīnque diēbus **urbs capta est.**	The city was captured *within five days*.

ABLATIVE OF MEANS OR INSTRUMENT (BY)

This ablative, without a preposition, expresses the means or instrument by which an action is performed.

| **Urbem *gladiīs* vincunt.** | They conquer the city *with swords*. |

ABLATIVE OF CAUSE (FROM)

This ablative, without a preposition, expresses the cause of an action.

| *Dolōre* **clamat.** | He shouts *because of pain*. |

ABLATIVE OF PERSONAL AGENT (BY)

This ablative, with the preposition **ā/ab**, expresses the agent through whom an action in the passive voice has been performed.

| **Urbs *ā mīlitibus* vincta est.** | The city was conquered *by the soldiers*. |

| **Liber *ā poētā* scrībētur.** | The book will be written *by the poet*. |

Note: The soldiers and the poet are *personal* agents, that is, people. For nonpersonal agents, Latin uses the ablative of means:

| **Urbs *avāritiā* dēlēta est.** | The city was destroyed *by avarice*. |

ABLATIVE OF MANNER (WITH)

This ablative, with the preposition **cum**, expresses the manner in which an action is performed.

***Cum gaudiō* canēbat.**	He was singing *with joy*.

However, if the ablative noun is modified by an adjective, the preposition **cum** becomes optional:

Magnō gaudiō	
Cum magnō gaudiō canēbat.	He sang *with great joy*.
Magnō cum gaudiō[1]	

ABLATIVE OF SEPARATION (FROM)

This ablative, like the ablative of place from which, expresses separation.

Tē līberābō *metū*.	I will free you *from fear*.
Vacuī *culpā* nōn sunt mortuī.	The dead are not free *from blame*.

ABLATIVE OF COMPARISON (FROM)

This ablative is used with a comparative adjective (see p. 24) and without a preposition to express that to which something is being compared.

Amor dūrior est *amīcitiā*.	Love is harder *than friendship*.

ABLATIVE OF DEGREE OF DIFFERENCE (BY)

This ablative is used with a comparative adjective to express, as the name suggests, the degree of difference in the comparison.

Amor *multō* dūrior est amīcitiā.	Love is harder than friendship *by much*.
Hic altior *tribus pedibus* est quam ille.	This man is taller than that man *by three feet*.

ABLATIVE OF DESCRIPTION (WITH)

A noun and adjective in the ablative case can describe another noun.

vir *grandibus pedibus*	a man *with large feet*
fēmina *magnā sapientiā*	a woman *of great wisdom*

This usage is similar to the genitive of description (see p. 81).

---

[1] Sometimes an adjective will move in front of a one-syllable preposition like this to give the expression a more pleasing and symmetrical form.

ABLATIVE OF RESPECT

This ablative is used to specify or limit a statement.

Illōs *virtūte* praecēdimus.   We surpass those men *in respect to
                                              excellence.*

ABLATIVE ABSOLUTE

An ablative noun and participle or two ablative nouns or adjectives may be used in combination to create what is essentially a subordinate clause.

Mīlitibus clamantibus, **rēx ad**   *With the soldiers shouting*, the king
   urbem ambulat.   walks toward the city.
Multīs **urbibus ā rēge** *captīs*,   *With many cities having been captured
by*
   populus timēbat.   the king, the people were afraid.
Rēge dēmentī, **mīlitēs timēbant.**   *With the king being crazy*, the soldiers
                                               were afraid.

(For a fuller treatment of this construction, see pp. 145–146.)

ABLATIVE WITH PREPOSITIONS

Many other ideas are expressed by the accusative with different prepositions (see p. 75).

Exercises

   7.   Translate the following. Then identify the italicized usages.

        1. Animal est grandius *puerō*.

           _____

        2. Animālia ā *puerō* dūcuntur.

           _____

        3. Fēminae *magnā cūrā* ad mare vēnērunt.

           _____

        4. Fēminae *Rōmā* vēnērunt

           _____

        5. *Avāritiā* poētam expulistis.

           _____

        6. *Gladiō* poētam expulistī.

           _____

        7. *Poētīs canentibus*, dī nōs audiēbant.

           _____

        8. *Illō annō* multa bella in terrā erant.

           _____

        9. Rēx *multō* dēmentior est rēgīnā.

           _____

10. Animālia *magnīs cornibus* timeō.

_____

11. *Timōre* ex urbe rēgīna cucurrit.

_____

8. Translate the following sentences:

1. Sunt enim optimō animō, summō cōnsiliō, singulārī concordiā.

_____

_____

2. Hī omnēs linguā, institūtīs, lēgibus inter sē differunt.

_____

_____

3. Sed Antōnius tenētur, premitur, urgētur nunc eīs cōpiīs quās iam habēmus, mox eīs quās paucīs diēbus novī cōsulēs comparābunt.

_____

_____

_____

4. Quis enim hōc adulescente castior, quis modestior, quod in iuventūte habēmus illustrius exemplum veteris sanctitātis?

_____

_____

_____

5. Attulerat iam ille līberae cīvitātī partim metū partim patientiā consuetūdinem serviendī. Cum illō egō tē dominandī cupīditāte conferre possum, cēterīs vērō rēbus nullō modō comparandus es.

_____

_____

_____

_____

_____

6. His auctōribus et ducibus, dīs iuvantibus, nōbīs vigilantibus et multum in posterum prōvidentibus, populō Rōmānō consentiente, erimus profectō līberī brevī tempore. Iūcundiōrem autem faciet lībertātem servitūtis recordātiō.

_____

_____

_____

_____

_____

_____

_____

Vocabulary

enim	for indeed
animus, -ī, m.	mind, spirit
summus, -a, -um	the highest, best
cōnsilium, -ī, n.	advice, planning
singulāris, -e	remarkable, outstanding
concordia, -ae, f.	agreement
lingua, -ae, f.	tongue, language
institūtum, -ī, n.	custom, usage
lex, lēgis, f.	law
differō	differ
urgeō, urgēre	press upon
cōpiae, -ārum, f.	troops
mox (adv.)	soon
consul, -is, m.	consul
comparō, comparāre	prepare, make ready
verbum, -ī, n.	word
appellō, appellāre	call
castus, -a, -um	chaste
modestus, -a, -um	modest
iuventūs, -tūtis, f.	youth
illustris, -e	shining, illustrious
vetus, veteris	old, ancient
sanctitās, -tātis, f.	moral purity, sanctity
cīvitās, -tātis, f.	citizenry, state
partim (adv.)	partly
patientia, -ae, f.	patience, suffering
consuetūdō, -tūdinis, f.	habit
serviō, servīre	to be a slave
cupīditās, -tātis, f.	greed
dominor, dominārī, dominātus sum	rule absolutely, dominate
conferō	compare
auctor, -ōris, m.	creator, producer
dux, ducis, m.	leader
iuvō, iuvāre	help, assist
vigilō, vigilāre	keep watch
in posterum	for the future

prōvideō, prōvidēre	provide
consentiō, consentīre	be in agreement
profectō (adv.)	without question
brevis, -e	brief, short
iūcundus, -a, -um	pleasing
autem	moreover
recordātiō, -ōnis, f.	recollection, memory
lībertās, -tātis, f.	liberty
servitūs, -tūtis, f.	slavery

Locative Case

The locative case expresses location. It is an older case that, for the most part, has died out in the language but survives in the names of cities, towns, islands, and the nouns **domus** and **rūs**.

Except for these instances, location is usually expressed by the ablative case without the preposition **in**.

CHAPTER 7

Syntax of the Adjective

The function of an adjective is to modify a noun. To do so, it must agree with the noun in gender, number, and case.

Generally, adjectives follow the nouns that they modify.

Poēta *dēmēns magnō* gaudiō lūnam *frīgidam* videt.
The insane poet sees the cold moon with great joy.

Note that the adjective **magnō** precedes its noun **gaudiō**. This is commonly the case with adjectives denoting quantity rather than quality. For example, Latin will use **multa pecūnia** rather than **pecūnia multa**.

This is also the case with demonstrative and interrogative adjectives:

quis vir?   what man?
ille vir   that man

Predicate Adjective

Sometimes an adjective is used in an equation or assertion. It must still agree with its noun.

Ventus est *magnus*.   The wind is great.

If a group of nouns is mixed masculine and feminine, the adjective will take the masculine.

Virī et fēminae sunt *miserī*.   The men and women are wretched.

Substantive Adjective

Sometimes an adjective does not modify a noun but stands alone as if it were itself a noun. This is called the *substantive* use of the adjective.[1]

***Bonus** ad mare ambulat.*	*The good man* walks to the water.

It is translated on the basis of its gender and number, here masculine singular—hence the good *man*.

***Bonae** ad mare ambulant.*	*The good women* walk to the water.
bonus, malus, et dēformis	the good (man), the bad (man), and the ugly (man)

Adverbial Use of the Adjective

Sometimes an adjective, rather than saying something general about a noun, will say something about that noun that is true only for the sentence in which it occurs. It seems to function more as an adverb.

Ille vir, cum hoc audīvit, *sapiēns* discessit.	That man, when he heard this, *wisely* departed.

Often such a usage will occur in the nominative case, modifying the subject, and often it will occur near the verb, i.e., in an *adverbial* position. Notice the difference:

***Sapiēns,** cum hoc audīvit, discessit.*	*The wise man*, when he heard this, departed.

Comparative and Superlative Adjectives

The comparative or superlative degree of the adjective may be used alone as a strengthened form of the positive.

Pater est *sapientior.*	The father is *very wise*.
Pater est *sapientissimus.*	The father is *extremely wise*.

Comparative adjectives often occur with an ablative of comparison nearby (see p. 93).

Pater est sapientior *filiō.*	The father is *wiser than the son*.

Comparative adjectives may also express a comparison using the adverb **quam**.

Pater est sapientior *quam filius.*	The father is wiser *than the son (is)*.

---

[1] "Substantive" is another term for noun.

When **quam** is used, both terms in the comparison must be in the same case: **fīlius** on page 100 is nominative to correspond with **pater**.

Dīcō *patrem* **sapientiōrem esse   quam** *fīlium.*

I say that *the father* is wiser than *the son*.

Here **fīlium** is accusative, to correspond to **patrem**, itself the subject of an indirect statement.

Superlative adjectives often take a partitive genitive.

Pecūnia est pessima *omnium malōrum.*   Money is the worst *of all evil things.*

Sometimes the superlative will occur with **quam** to express the adjective's meaning "as strongly as possible."

Pater est *quam sapientissimus.*   The father is *as wise as possible.*

Exercises

1. Translate the following.

1. Malī pecūniam amant.

   _____

2. Multa pecūnia est multō melior amōre.

   _____

3. Multa pecūnia est multō melior quam multus amor.

   _____

4. Aurum pulcherrimum omnium bonōrum est.

   _____

5. Dīcō aquam esse quam pulcherrimam.

   _____

6. Poēta miser dē avāritiā Rōmānōrum clāmābat.

   _____

7. Poēta dē avāritiā Rōmānōrum miser clāmābat.

   _____
   _____

2. Translate the following.

1. Lūce sunt clāriōra nōbīs tua cōnsilia omnia.

   _____
   _____
   _____

2. Hanc vērō taeterrimam bēluam quis ferre potest?

_____

_____

_____

3. Habet quidem certē rēs pūblica adulēscentīs nōbilissimōs parātōs dēfensōrēs.

_____

_____

4. Quis clāriōribus virīs quōdam tempore iūcundior, quis turpiōribus coniunctior? Quis cīvis meliōrum partium aliquandō, quis taetrior hostis huic cīvitātī? Quis in voluptātibus inquinātior, quis in labōribus patientior? Quis in rapācitāte avārior, quis in largītiōne effūsior?

_____

_____

_____

_____

_____

_____

_____

_____

_____

Vocabulary

lux, lūcis, f.	light
clārus, -a, -um	clear, bright
cōnsilium, -ī, n.	advice, planning
taeter, -tra, -trum	horrible, foul
bēlua, -ae, f.	beast
quidem (adv.)	indeed
adulescēns, -ntis	young, youthful
parō, parāre	prepare
dēfensor, -ōris, m.	defender
iūcundus, -a, -um	pleasing
turpis, -e	foul
coniunctus, -a, um	conjoined
aliquandō (adv.)	ever, at any time
hostis, -is, -ium, m.	enemy
cīvitās, -tātis, f.	citizenry, state
voluptās, -tātis, f.	pleasure
inquinātus, -a, -um	dirty, stained

labor, -ōris, m.	labor, work
rapācitās, -tātis, f.	rapacity
avārus, -a, -um	greedy
largītiō, -ōnis, f.	extravagant expenditure, bribery
effūsus, -a, -um	unrestrained

Syntax of the Simple Sentence

A simple sentence is an *independent* clause; that is, unlike a subordinate clause, it can stand alone as a complete unit of meaning. This is what makes a sentence.

Most simple sentences have a subject and a verb:

Vir ambulat.   The man walks.

In Latin the subject may be implied in the verb by its ending:

Ambulā*mus*.   *We* walk.

Sometimes the verb "to be" may be left out of a sentence:

Ille vir sapiens.   That man is wise.

Because Latin is an inflected language, it does not rely upon word order to determine the grammatical meaning of its phrases and sentences. This does not mean that its word order is random.

Latin has a normal, neutral order that tends to place the subject of a sentence first and the verb last. Usually direct objects and adverbs gravitate toward the verb, with other information such as datives and prepositional phrases falling in the middle of the sentence.

Consider the following sequence:

Dēlet.	He destroys.
Mīlitēs dēlent.	The soldiers destroy.
Mīlitēs urbem dēlēbunt.	The soldiers will destroy the city.
Mīlitēs gladiīs urbem dēlēbant.	The soldiers were destroying the city with swords.
Mīlitēs cum nautīs gladiīs urbem prō rēge dēlēverant.	The soldiers with the sailors had destroyed the city with swords on behalf of the king.

Remember that adjectives and genitives tend to follow the nouns they modify:

Mīlitēs rēgnī audācēs gladiīs magnīs urbem miserrimam prō rēge caecō dēlēvērunt.

The bold soldiers of the kingdom destroyed the most wretched city with great swords on behalf of the blind king.

Exercise

1. Translate the following.

1. Nauta videt.

2. Nauta montem vidēbit.

   _____

3. Nauta oculīs montem vīdit.

   _____

4. Nauta bellum in montibus oculīs vīderat.

   _____

5. Multīs cum lacrimīs nauta miser bellum pessimum in montibus rēgnī vidēbat.

   _____

   _____

   _____

6. Mōns vidētur.

7. Mōns ā nautā vidētur.

   _____

8. Bellum ā nautā in montibus vīsum est.

   _____

   _____

Indicative Mood

The indicative is the mood of fact. It presents information simply as true. (Tenses of the indicative should be translated according to the paradigms given in Chapter 2.)

Exercises

2. Translate the following sentences, paying particular attention to the tense of the verb.

1. Rēx cīvēs terret.

   _____

2. Rēx cīvēs terrēbit.

   _____

3. Rēx cīvēs terruit.

_____

4. Rēx cīvēs terruerit.

_____

5. Rēx cīvēs terruerat.

_____

6. Rēx cīvēs terrēbat.

_____

3.   Translate the following.

1. Argūmentīs agēmus, signīs lūce omnī clāriōribus crīmina refellēmus; rēs cum rē, causa cum causā, ratiō cum ratiōne pugnābit.

_____
_____
_____
_____

2. Hōrum duōrum crīminum videō auctōrem, videō fontem, videō certum nōmen et caput.

_____
_____
_____

3. Vērum haec genera virtūtum nōn sōlum in mōribus nostrīs sed vix iam in librīs reperiuntur. Chartae quoque quae illam pristinam sevēitātem continēbant obsolēvērunt.

_____
_____
_____
_____

Vocabulary

argūmentum, -ī, n.	argument
agō, agere, ēgī, āctus	act, proceed
signum, -ī, n.	sign, proof
lux, lūcis, f.	light
clārus, -a, -um	clear, bright
crīmen, crīminis, n.	criminal charge
rēs reī, f.	(here) fact
causa, -ae, f.	case

refellō, refellere	refute, disprove
ratiō, -ōnis, f.	reasoning, reckoning
auctor, -ōris, m.	source, creator
fōns, -ntis, -ium, m.	fountain, source
caput, capitis, n.	head
vērum	but
genus, generis, n.	type, kind
virtūs, -tūtis, f.	excellence
mōs, mōris, -ium, m.	custom
vix (adv.)	scarcely
liber, librī, m.	book
reperiō, reperīre	discover
charta, -ae, f.	page
quoque	even, also
pristinus, -a, -um	ancient, pristine
sevēritās, -tātis, f.	severity, seriousness
contineō, continēre	contain
obsolescō, obsolescere	fall into disuse, become forgotten

Exercise

4. Translate the following passage.

Inter terram caelumque [in] eōdem spīritū pendent certīs discrēta spatiīs septem sīdera quae ab incessū vocāmus errantia. Eōrum medius sōl fertur, amplissimā magnitūdine ac potestāte nec temporum modo terrārumque, sed sīderum etiam ipsōrum caelīque rector. Hunc esse mundī tōtius animum ac mentem, hunc principāle nātūrae regimen ac nūmen crēdere decet opera eius aestimantēs. Hic lūcem rēbus ministrat aufertque tenebrās, hic reliqua sīdera occultat, illustrat; hic vicēs temporum annumque semper renascentem ex usū nātūrae temperat; hic caelī tristitiam discutit atque etiam hūmānī nūbila animī serēnat; hic suum lūmen cēterīs quoque sīderibus faenerat, praeclārus, eximius, omnia intuēns, omnia etiam exaudiēns. . .

_____

_____

_____

_____

_____

Vocabulary

terra, -ae, f.	earth, land
caelum, -ī, n.	heaven
spīritus, -ūs, m.	breath, air
pendeō, pendēre	hang
certus, -a, -um	certain
discrētus, -a, -um	separate
spatiam, -ī, n.	space, interval
septem	seven
sīdus, sīderis, n.	star
incessus, -ūs, m.	walking, movement
vocō, vocāre	call
errō, errāre	wander (here errantia = planets)
medius, -a, -um	in the middle, central
sōl, sōlis, m.	sun
fertur	(here) moves
amplus, -a, -um	large
magnitūdō, -inis, f.	size, magnitude
potestās, -tātis, f.	power
tempus, temporis, n.	time, season
rector, -ōris, m.	helmsman, ruler
mundus, -ī, m.	world
principālis, -e	original, principal

regimen, -inis, n.	rule
nūmen, -inis, n.	spirit
crēdō, crēdere	believe
decet	it is fitting (+acc. and inf.)
opus, operis, n.	work
aestimō, aestimāre	judge, reckon, estimate
lux, lūcis, f.	light
ministrō, ministrāre	serve, provide
auferō	remove
tenebrae, -ārum, f. pl.	darkness, shadows
reliquus, -a, -um	remaining
occultō, occultāre	hide, conceal
illustrō, illustrāre	illuminate
vicis, vicis, f.	turning, succession
annus, -ī, m.	year
renascor, renascī, renātus sum	be reborn
temperō, temperāre	restrain, regulate
tristitia, -ae, f.	gloom, sadness
discutiō, discutere	strike away, scatter
nūbila, -ōrum, n. pl.	clouds
serēnō, serēnāre	make calm, pacify
lūmen, -inis, n.	light
faenerō, faenerāre	lend
praeclārus, -a, -um	extremely bright
eximius, -a, -um	outstanding
intueor, intuērī	look upon, watch

Imperative Mood

As stated earlier, the imperative is the mood for giving commands. It should be translated according to the paradigms given in Chapter 2.

tacēte	be silent (pl.)
abī	go away

NEGATIVE COMMANDS

For negative commands, Latin does not simply negate the imperative, but it uses a combination of **nōlī** for the singular or **nōlīte** for the plural with the present infinitive.

Nōlī ambulāre!	Do not walk! (sing.)
Nōlīte loquī!	Do not speak! (pl.)
Nōlī vidērī!	Do not be seen! (sing.)

Latin also expresses negative commands using either the present or perfect subjunctive with the negative **nē**:

Nē ambulēs!	Do not walk! (sing.)
Nē ambulāveris	Do not walk! (sing.)
Nē interficiātis!	Do not kill! (pl.)
Nē interfēceritis	Do not kill! (pl.)

Exercises

5. Translate the following.

   1. Nōlīte clamāre!

   2. Nē librum scrībās!

   3. Nē fīlium pepuleris!

   4. Nōlīte pellī!

   5. Nē urbem dēlēveritis, o mīlitēs!

   6. Nōlīte urbem dēlēre, o mīlitēs!

   7. Urbem dēlēte, o mīlitēs!

   8. Urbem dēlē, o militēs!

6. Translate the following.

   1. Audīte, audīte, patrēs conscriptī, et cognōscite reī pūblicae vulnera.

   2. Conservāte igitur reī pūblicae, iūdicēs, cīvem bonārum artium, bonārum partium, bonōrum virōrum.

3. Nē mē hodiē, cum istī ut prōvocāvit responderō, oblītum esse putētis meī.

_____

_____

4. Quam ob rem discēde atque nunc mihi timōrem ēripe: si est vērus, nē opprimar, sīn falsus, ut tandem aliquandō timēre dēsinam.

_____

_____

_____

_____

Vocabulary

patrēs conscriptī	senators
cognōscō, cognōscere	learn
vulnis, vulneris, n.	wound
conservō, conservāre	save, preserve
igitur (adv.)	therefore
iūdex, iūdicis, m.	judge
cīvis, cīvis, -ium, m.	citizen
ars, artis, -ium, f.	skill, art
pars, partis, -ium, f.	part
hodiē (adv.)	today
prōvocō, prōvocāre	provoke
respondeō, respondēre	respond
oblīviscor, oblīviscī, oblītus sum	forget
putō, putāre	think
quam ob rem	for which reason
discēdo, discēdere	leave, depart
timor, -ōris, m.	fear
ēripiō, ēripere	tear away, remove
vērus, -a, -um	true, real
opprimō, opprimere	oppress
sīn	but if
falsus, -a, -um	false, unreal
tandem (adv.)	finally, at least
aliquandō	at some time, ever
timeō, timēre	fear
dēsinō, dēsinere	cease (+inf.)

Subjunctive Mood: Independent Uses

Chapter 2 stated that the subjunctive should not be translated in isolation, but that its translation often involved such English words as "could," "would," and "might."

The subjunctive mood does most of its work in subordinate clauses, usually governed by conjunctions or a grammatical context that determines its meaning. (These will be treated in the next chapter.) However, the subjunctive can also be used as the main verb of an independent clause. Following are its main independent uses.

POTENTIAL

The subjunctive may express potentiality or possibility. The present tense is used for present potentiality, and the imperfect for past potentiality:

Mīlitēs urbem dēleant.	The soldiers could destroy the city.
Mīlitēs urbem dēlērent.	The soldiers could have destroyed the city.

DELIBERATIVE

This form of the subjunctive is used, often in the first person, to ask questions not of fact but of deliberation:

Urbem dēleāmus?	Should we destroy the city?
Quid[1] urbem dēlērēmus?	Why should we have destroyed the city?

Again the present subjunctive is used for deliberation in present time, and the imperfect subjunctive for past deliberation.

OPTATIVE

The optative subjunctive expresses a wish. Often the word **utinam**, "if only," accompanies this usage.[2]

The present subjunctive expresses a wish in the present time:

Utinam mīlitēs urbem dēleant!	If only the soldiers would destroy the city!

The imperfect subjunctive also expresses a wish in the present time, but one that cannot come true:

Utinam mīlitēs urbem dēlērent!	If only the soldiers were destroying the city! (We know that they are not.)

---

[1] **Quid** here is an adverbial accusative, a common usage best translated as "why?"
[2] Less often, **ut** may be used.

The pluperfect subjunctive expresses a wish in the past that could not have come true:

Utinam mīlitēs urbem dēlēvissent!   If only the soldiers had destroyed the city! (We know that they did not.)

To negate an optative subjunctive, Latin uses **nē** rather than **nōn**:

Utinam nē canant!   If only they were not singing!

HORTATORY OR JUSSIVE

The subjunctive can be used to express commands, mostly in the first and third persons.[3] (For second-person commands, usually the imperative is used.)
Generally the present subjunctive is used:

Urbem dēleāmus!   Let us destroy the city!
Mīlitēs urbem dēleant!   Let the soldiers destroy the city!

To negate these, Latin uses **nē**.

Nē loquātur!   Let him not speak.

Exercises

7. Translate the following. Then identify the italicized usages.

1. Utinam nautae nostrī *vīcissent!*

---

2. Ut nautae *vincant!*

---

3. Nautae *vincant.*

---

4. Ad mare *ambulem?*

---

5. Ad mare *ambulārēmus?*

---
[3] Customarily the first-person usage is called *hortatory* and the third-person *jussive.*

6. Ad mare *ambulēmus*!

_____

_____

7. Utinam ad mare *ambulāvissēmus*!

_____

_____

8. Mīlitēs ad mare nōn *ambulārent*?

_____

_____

8. Translate the following.

1. Ad decus et ad lībertātem nātī sumus: aut haec teneāmus aut cum dīgnitāte moriāmur.

_____

_____

2. Quis enim nōn timeat omnia prōvidentem et cōgitantem et animadvertentem et omnia ad sē pertinēre putantem curiōsum et plēnum negōtiī deum?

_____

_____

_____

_____

3. O stultitiam! Stultitiamne dīcam an impudentiam singulārem?

_____

4. Dētur aliquī lūdus aetātī sit adulescentia līberior; nōn omnia voluptātibus dēnegentur; nōn semper superet vēra illa et dērecta ratiō; vincat aliquandō cupiditās voluptāsque ratiōnem.

_____

_____

_____

_____

5. Utinam tam facile vēra invenīre possim quam falsa convincere!

_____

6. Utinam cum Caesar societātem aut numquam coissēs aut numquam dirēmissēs!

_____

7. Quid enim mē interpōnerem audāciae tuae?

Vocabulary

decus, decoris, n.	honor
lībertās, -tātis, f.	freedom
aut...aut	either...or
nascor, nascī, nātus sum	be born
dīgnitās, -tātis, f.	dignity, prestige
enim	for indeed
prōvideō, prōvidēre	foresee, provide
cōgitō, cōgitāre	think, ponder
animadvertō, animadvertere	notice
pertineō, pertinēre	extend to, relate to
putō, putāre	think
curiōsus, -a, -um	careful, attentive
plēnus, -a, -um	full
negōtium, -ī, n.	business, concern
stultitia, -ae, f.	stupidity
impudentia, -ae, f.	shamelessness
singulāris, -e	singular, remarkable
lūdus, -ī, m.	sport, gaming
aetās, -tātis, f.	age, time of life
adulescentia, -ae, f.	youth
līber, lībera, līberum	free
voluptās, -tātis, f.	pleasure
dēnegō, dēnegāre	deny, refuse
superō, superāre	overcome
vērus, -a, -um	true, real
dērectus, -a, -um	upright, straight
ratiō, -ōnis, f.	reason, reckoning
vincō, vincere	conquer
aliquandō (adv.)	sometimes
cupiditās, -tātis, f.	desire

falsus, -a, -um	false
convincō, convincere	defeat, refute
societās, -tātis, f.	alliance
numquam (adv.)	never
coeō, coīre	enter
dirimō, dirimere, dirēmī, diremptus	rip apart, destroy
interpōnō, interponere	place as an obstacle, interpose

Participles

Participles are defined as verbal adjectives. That is, they combine features of adjectives and verbs.

As adjectives, they modify nouns and must agree with the nouns they modify in gender, number, and case. They may also be used as substantives.

poēta canēns	the singing poet
urbs capta	the captured city
captus	the captured man

As verbs they show tense—present, perfect, or future—and voice—active or passive.

They may also govern direct objects and take many constructions of finite verbs.

| **Poēta lūnam *vidēns* canit.** | The poet *seeing* the moon sings. |

Here **lūnam** is the direct object of the participle **vidēns**, which itself modifies the subject **poēta**.

Often, as in the above example, the participle separates itself from the noun it modifies in order to enclose anything it governs—in this case, the direct object **lūnam**.

| **Mīles urbem a rēge *captam dēlētūrus* clāmat.** | The soldier *about to destroy* the city *captured* by the king shouts. |

Note how **a rēge** is enclosed by **urbem captam**, which is itself enclosed by **mīles dēlētūrus**.

Because participles do so much work in Latin, it is often useful to translate them more fully as relative clauses in English:

The soldier *who is about to destroy* the *city which was captured* by the king is shouting.

It is important to realize, however, that the tense of a participle is not an independent time value as it is for forms of the indicative, but is only relative to the tense of the main verb in its clause.

The time value of a present participle is simultaneous with that of the main verb:

| **Poēta *canēns* lūnam videt.** | The poet *who is singing* sees the moon. |

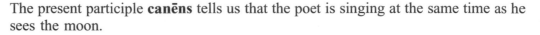

The present participle **canēns** tells us that the poet is singing at the same time as he sees the moon.

Poēta *canēns* **lūnam vidēbat.**	The poet *who was singing* saw the moon.

Now the time value of the present participle must be simultaneous with that of the main verb, which is in the past, **vidēbat**, and so it is translated "who was singing."

The time value of the perfect participle is prior to that of the main verb:

Mīles urbem a rēge *captam* **dēlet.**	The soldier destroys the city *which was captured* by the king.

The perfect participle **captam** tells us that the capture took place prior to the action of the main verb **dēlet**.

If the main verb is itself in the past tense, the perfect participle will express a time prior to that time:

Mīles urbem a rēge *captam* **dēlēvit.**	The soldier destroyed the city *which had been conquered* by the king.

If the main verb is in the future, the perfect participle will again express a time prior to that:

Mīles urbem a rēge *captam* **dēlēbit.**	The soldier will destroy the city *which has been captured* by the king.

The time value of the future active participle is subsequent to that of the main verb:

Mīles urbem *dēlētūrus* **clāmat.**	The soldier *who is going to destroy* the city is shouting.

The destruction denoted by **dēlētūrus** will take place after the present time signified by **clāmat**.

Mīles urbem *dēlētūrus* **clāmāvit.**	The soldier *who was about to destroy* the city shouted.

Exercise

9. Translate the following.

1. poēta canēns

   _____

2. lībertās dēlēta

   _____

3. lībertās avāritiā dēlēta

   _____

4. lībertās avāritiā mīlitum dēlēta

   _____

5. poēta clāmātūrus

   _____

6. poēta in monte clāmātūrus

_____

7. poēta in monte dē lībertāte clāmātūrus

_____

8. poēta in monte dē lībertāte avāritiā mīlitum dēlētā clāmātūrus.

_____
_____

9. Poēta in monte dē lībertāte avāritiā mīlitum dēlētā clāmatūrus moritur.

_____
_____

10. Poēta in monte dē lībertāte avāritiā mīlitum dēlētā clāmatūrus mortuus est.

_____
_____

11. Puer ad mare ambulāns servōs captōs timet.

_____
_____

12. Puer ad mare ambulāns servōs ā nautīs captōs timēbat.

_____
_____

13. Puer ad mare ambulāns servōs animālia interficientēs videt.

_____
_____

14. Puer ad mare ambulāns animālia a servīs interfecta vīdit.

_____
_____

Relative Clauses

Relative clauses, like participle phrases, are both adjectival and govern grammatical constructions themselves. They are adjectival in that they modify an _antecedent_ to which they are attached by a relative pronoun. The relative pronoun must agree with its antecedent in gender and number. It takes its case from the grammatical function it fulfills within its own clause.

Rēx _quem poēta timet_ **pecūniam amat.**   The king _whom the poet fears_ loves money.

Most often a relative clause begins with a relative pronoun and ends with a verb:

quem poēta timet

The relative pronoun **quem** is masculine accusative singular. Its antecedent **rēx** is masculine nominative singular. The pronoun **quem** is masculine and singular to agree with **rēx**, and accusative because it is the direct object of the verb **timet** within its own clause.

Rēx *cui gladium dedistī* **ā poētā timētur.**

The king *to whom you gave* a sword is feared by the poet.

In agreement with its antecedent **rēx**, **cui** is masculine singular. It is dative because it is the indirect object of its own clause.

If it can be easily understood in context, the antecedent of a relative pronoun may be left out:

Quī pecūniam amant sunt miserī.

Those who love money are wretched.

The antecedent of **quī** is understood to be the subject of the main verb **sunt**.

Exercise

10. Translate the following. Explain the case of the relative pronoun.

1. Rēgīna quam rēx timet ā poētā amātur.

_____

_____

2. Rēx a quō rēgīna timētur poētam ōdit.

_____

_____

3. Rēx quem rēgīna ōdit animālia magnōrum cornuum timet.

_____

_____

4. Animālia quae ad urbem ducta erant ā rēge quī poētās ōdit multum timēbantur.

_____

_____

5. Animālia quibus cornua magna erant a mīlitibus rēgis interfecta sunt.

_____

_____

6. Corpora animālium quōrum cornua vendita erant in ignī pōnēbantur.

_____

_____

CHAPTER 9

Syntax of the Complex Sentence

A complex sentence is one that contains one or more subordinate clauses that are said to depend on the main or *independent* clause. This means that they cannot stand alone as sentences, but must exist in conjunction with an independent clause.

When he got home, he destroyed the television.

Because he destroyed the television, his sister was angry.

"When he got home" and "because he destroyed the television" are subordinate clauses. They cannot stand alone as sentences. A subordinate clause gives more information about the main clause by relating it to other circumstances.

We say that words such as "when" and "because" are *subordinating conjunctions*. They serve to introduce subordinate clauses and usually tell you what clauses mean.

"When" introduces a *temporal* clause. "When he got home" is a temporal clause. It situates the action of the main clause in time, telling us *when* he destroyed the television.

"Because" introduces a *causal* clause. "Because he destroyed the television" is a causal clause, telling us *why* his sister was angry.

Latin has many different kinds of subordinate clauses. They are categorized according to the different kinds of information they offer about the main clause. Although there are many such categories, it may be convenient to simply think of their differences as differences in the vocabulary of subordinating conjunctions.

Some subordinating conjunctions take the indicative, and some take the subjunctive. Some can take either, with differences in meaning. Those that take the indicative will take whatever tense their sense requires. Those that take the subjunctive, however, are bound by two important grammatical considerations, known as *sequence of tenses* and *relative time*. These will apply to almost *all* uses of the subjunctive in subordinate clauses:

Sequence of Tenses

Subordinate uses of the subjunctive follow the "sequence of tenses." This means that the tense of the subjunctive used in a subordinate clause will depend on the tense of the verb in the main clause.

There are four tenses of the subjunctive:

Present

Imperfect

Perfect

Pluperfect

If the main verb refers to the present or future, the subjunctive in a subordinate clause that follows it must be either present or perfect. This is said to be in *primary sequence*. If the main verb refers to the past, the subjunctive in a subordinate clause that follows it must be either imperfect or pluperfect. This is said to be in *secondary sequence*.[1]

In each sequence, then, there are two possible tenses of the subjunctive that may be used. The difference between the two in each case will be one of relative time.

RELATIVE TIME

The concept of relative time first appeared in the discussion of participles (p. 117). There it was said that the tense of the participle is not an objective time value, but one that can be understood only in relation to the time of the main verb. The same is true of subjunctives in subordinate clauses.

In primary sequence, the present subjunctive expresses a time simultaneous with (or sometimes subsequent to) that of the main verb:

Sciō quid *faciās*.   I know what *you are doing*.

The present subjunctive tells us that whatever you are doing is happening at the same time as my knowing.

The perfect subjunctive expresses a time prior to that of the main verb:

Sciō quid *fēceris*.   I know what you *did*.

The perfect subjunctive tells us that what you did happened before the time of my knowing, as if to say "I now know what you did then."

---

[1] The perfect indicative is unusual in that it has potentially two different time values, one past ("did") and one present ("have done"). Because this is so, it may lead to primary or secondary sequence in a given context. However, this should be something to consider at more advanced stages of study.

In secondary sequence, the imperfect subjunctive expresses a time simultaneous with (sometimes subsequent to) that of the main verb:

Sciēbam quid *facerēs*.   I knew what you *were doing*.

The pluperfect subjunctive expresses a time prior to that of the main verb:

Sciēbam quid *fēcissēs*.   I knew what you *had done*.

As stated above, though there are many different categories of subordinate clauses, for the most part it is possible to handle them correctly by knowing what their subordinating conjunctions mean and remembering the rules of sequence for uses of the subjunctive.

Temporal Clauses

Temporal clauses situate the action of the main clause in time by relating it to something else. There are many different subordinating conjunctions that introduce them.

Some temporal conjunctions take the indicative:

postquam	after
cum	when
ut	when
ubi	when

Cum mīlitēs urbem vīcērunt,   When the soldiers conquered the town,
    servī fūgērunt.   the slaves fled.

Some can take the indicative or subjunctive:

antequam	before
priusquam	before
dum	until
dōnec	until
quoad	until

They take the indicative to represent facts:

Poētae fūgērunt antequam mīlitēs   The poets fled before the soldiers
    urbem *cēpērunt*.   *captured* the city.

The Latin tells us that the capture of the city actually took place.

Mīlitēs pugnābant dōnec poētae   The soldiers fought until the poets fled.
    fūgērunt.

These conjunctions take the subjunctive to represent something foreseen or anticipated:

Pōetae fūgērunt antequam mīlitēs urbem *caperent.*	The poets fled before the soldiers *could capture* the city.

The Latin tells us that the capture of the city is something anticipated by the poets. It does not tell us whether or not it actually took place.

The imperfect subjunctive is used here because the main verb **fūgērunt** refers to the past, creating secondary sequence. In primary sequence, the present subjunctive would be used:

Poētae fugient antequam mīlitēs urbem *capiant.*	The poets will flee before the soldiers *can capture* the city.

Causal Clauses

A causal clause gives the cause for the main clause.
Some conjunctions take the indicative:

quando	because
quoniam	because

Quoniam mīlitēs urbem *cēpērunt*, **poētae fūgērunt.**	Because the soldiers *captured* the city, the poets fled.

Some take the subjunctive:

cum	because

Cum mīlitēs urbem *cēpissent*, **poētae fūgērunt.**	Because the soldiers *had captured the city*, the poets fled.

The pluperfect subjunctive **cēpissent** is used in secondary sequence and shows time prior to the main verb.

The imperfect subjunctive would show time simultaneous:

Cum mīlitēs urbem *caperent*, **poētae fūgērunt.**	Because the soldiers *were capturing* the city, the poets fled.

In primary sequence the present subjunctive shows time simultaneous:

Cum mīlitēs urbem *capiant*, **poētae fugiunt.**	Because the soldiers *are capturing* the city, the poets are fleeing.

The perfect subjunctive shows time prior:

Cum mīlitēs urbem *cēperint*, **poētae fūgiunt.**	Because the soldiers *have captured* the city, the poets are fleeing.

Some conjunctions can take the indicative or the subjunctive:

quod   because
quia   because

They take the indicative to assert a cause as fact.

Quod mīlitēs urbem *cēpērunt*, poētae fūgērunt.

Because the soldiers *(actually) captured* the city, the poets fled.

They take the subjunctive to express a cause given by someone other than the writer of the sentence:

Poētae fūgērunt quod mīlitēs urbem *cēpissent*.

The poets fled (supposedly) because the soldiers had captured the city.

Concessive Clauses

Concessive clauses begin with the word "although." They *concede* that, although something is true, the main clause remains unaffected and is still true. Often the main clause will contain the word **tamen**, "nevertheless."

Some conjunctions take the indicative:

etsī   although

quamquam   although

Some take the subjunctive:

cum   although

quamvīs   although

Cum mīlitēs urbem *cēpissent*, poētae tamen nōn fūgērunt.

Although the soldiers *had captured* the city, the poets nevertheless did not flee.

The pluperfect subjunctive is used in secondary sequence, showing time prior to that of the main verb **fūgērunt**.

Exercises

1.   Translate the following. Pay close attention to the mood of the verb in the subordinate clauses.

1.   Quia servī miserrimī erant, rēx populō aurum dabat.

   _____

2.   Rēx populō aurum dabat quod servī miserrimī essent.

   _____

   _____

3. Etsī servī miserrimī sunt, aurum populō rēx nōn dōnābit.

_____

4. Cum rēx populō aurum dedisset, servī nōn clāmābant.

_____

5. Cum rēx populō aurum dedit, clāmāvērunt.

_____

6. Quoniam rēgīna capta erat, rēx bellum parābat.

_____

7. Rēx bellum parābat priusquam rēgīna interficerētur.

_____

8. Bellum gerēbant dōnec rēx interfectus est.

_____

9. Bellum gerēbant dum rēx redīret.

_____

10. Cum rēx interfectus esset, rēgīna clāmābat.

_____

11. Cum rēx interfectus esset, rēgīna tamen fēlix erat.

_____

12. Ut lūna discessit, lūx diēī vēnit.

_____

_____

2. Translate the following sentences.

1. Tum dēnique interficiēre, cum iam nēmō tam improbus, tam perditus, tam tuī similis invenīrī poterit.

_____

_____

2. Neque ideo minus efficācēs sunt oratiōnēs nostrae quia ad aurēs iūdicantium cum voluptāte perveniunt.

_____

_____

3. Nam interitus quidem tuī quis bonus nōn esset auctor, cum in eō salūs et vīta optimī cuiusque, līertās populī Rōmānī dīgnitāsque consisteret?

_____
_____
_____
_____

4. Sed antequam aggrediar ad ea quae a tē disputata sunt, dē tē ipsō dīcam quid sentiam.

_____
_____
_____

5. Cum dē antīquīs loquāris, ūtere antīqua lībertāte, ā quā vel magis dēgenerāvimus quam ab ēloquentiā.

_____
_____

6. Ipse Pompeius, ab inimīcīs Caesaris incitātus et quod nēminem dīgnitāte secum exaequārī volēbat, tōtum sē ab ēius amīcitiā āverterat.

_____
_____
_____

7. Vērum tamen hominēs, quamvīs in turbidīs rēbus sint, sī modo hominēs sunt, interdum animīs relaxantur.

_____
_____
_____

Vocabulary

tum (adv.)	then
dēnique (adv.)	finally, at last
interficiō, interficere	kill
nēmō, nēminis	nobody
improbus, -a, -um	base, depraved
perditus, -a, -um	ruined, desperate
similis, -e	similar (+ gen.)
ideō	for this reason
efficax, -ācis	effective
ōrātiō, -ōnis, f.	speech
auris, auris, -ium, f.	ear
iūdicō, iūdicāre	to judge
voluptās, -tātis, f.	pleasure

perveniō, pervenīre	arrive, come to
interitus, -ūs, m.	death, destruction
auctor, -ōris, m.	creator, producer
quidem	indeed
salūs, -ūtis, f.	health, safety
lībertās, -tātis, f.	freedom
dīgnitās, -tātis, f.	dignity, prestige
consistō, consistere	rest upon
aggredior, aggredī, aggressus sum	approach
disputō, disputāre	argue, dispute
antiquus, -a, -um	ancient, old
loquor, loquī, locūtus sum	speak
ūtor, ūtī, ūsus sum (+ abl.)	make use of
dēgenerō, dēgenerāre	degenerate
ēloquentia, -ae, f.	eloquence
Pompeius, -ī, m.	Pompeius
incitātus, -a, -um	roused, incited
inimīcus, -a, -um	enemy
Caesar, -aris, m.	Caesar
exaequō, exaequāre	make level or equal
amīcitia, -ae, f.	friendship
āvertō, āvertere	turn away
vērum	but
turbidus, -a, -um	violently disturbed
modo (adv.)	at least, only
interdum (adv.)	sometimes
animus, -ī, m.	mind, spirit
relaxō, relaxāre	relax

Purpose Clauses

Purpose clauses express the purpose or reason for an action. Like causal clauses, they answer the question "why?"

They are introduced by the conjunction **ut** or, if negated, by the conjunction **nē**, and they take the subjunctive according to the rules of sequence.

Mīlitēs urbem vincent *ut rēx capiātur.*   The soldiers will conquer the city *in order that the king may be captured.*

Mīlitēs urbe vīcērunt *nē rēx fugeret*.   The soldiers conquered the city *in order*
                                                 that the king might not flee.

Indirect Commands

Indirect commands follow verbs of commanding, requesting, begging, etc. They express the content of the command or request and answer the question "what," i.e., "what did he command?"

They are introduced by the conjunction **ut** and negated with **nē**, and take the subjunctive according to the rules of sequence.

Rēx imperat *ut mīlitēs urbem vincant*.   The king orders *that the soldiers*
                                                 conquer the city.
Rēx ōrābat *nē mīlitēs urbem vincerent*.   The king was begging *that the soldiers*
                                                 not conquer the city.

Result Clauses

Result clauses express the result of an action or state. They are introduced by **ut** and take the subjunctive according to the rules of sequence:

Tam miser est *ut clāmet*.   He is so wretched *that he shouts.*
Ita clāmāvit *ut pueri timērent*.   He shouted in such a way *that the*
                                                 children were afraid.

Usually the main clause before a result clause contains an intensifying word such as **ita** or **tam** that triggers the result.

Unlike purpose clauses and indirect commands, which also use the conjunction **ut**, result clauses do not use **nē** but are negated using **nōn** inside the clause:

Tam dulciter poēta canēbat ut   The poet sang so sweetly that we *were*
  loquī *nōn possēmus*.   *not able to speak.*

A result clause may also be the subject or object of certain verbs:

Rēx effēcit *ut lībertās dēlērētur*.   The king brought it about *that liberty*
                                                 was destroyed.

In this sentence the clause **ut lībertās dēlērētur** is actually the direct object of the verb **effēcit**.

Accidit *ut rēx dēmentissimus sit*.   It happens *that the king is extremely*
                                                 insane.

In this sentence the clause **ut rēx dēmentissimus sit** is the subject of the verb **accidit**. In such cases the clause is called a substantive result clause, because the clause acts as a noun within its sentence.

Fear Clauses

Fear clauses express fears. They use the conjunctions **ut** and **nē** but with reverse meanings from the clauses above. **Ut** expresses negative fears, and **nē** expresses positive fears.

Timēbāmus *nē* rēx lībertātem *dēlērēt*.	We were afraid *that* the king *would destroy* liberty.
Timēmus *ut* mīlitēs *veniant*.	We are afraid *that* the soldiers *are not coming*.

Sometimes a fear clause may begin with **nē** and then be negated with **nōn**:

Timēmus *nē* mīlitēs *nōn veniant*.	We are afraid *that* the soldiers *are not coming*.

Clauses of Prevention

Certain verbs with meanings of prevention or hindrance take clauses of prevention. They are introduced by the conjunction **nē** or **quōminus** and take the subjunctive according to the rules of sequence:

Rēx mīlitēs impedīvit *quōminus urbem caperent*.	The king prevented the soldiers *from capturing the city*.

If the main clause is negated, the prevention clause may be introduced by **quīn**:

Rēx nōn impediet *quīn mīlitēs urbem capiant*.	The king will not prevent *the soldiers from capturing the city*.

Clauses of Doubting

Doubt is expressed in two ways in Latin. If the expression of doubt is not negated, it will take the form of an indirect question (see p. 153). If the expression of doubt is negated, it takes a clause of doubting introduced by the conjunction **quīn**:

Nōn dubitō *quīn mīlitēs urbem cēperint*.	I do not doubt *that the soldiers captured the city*.

In this example the perfect subjunctive expresses time prior to that of the main verb in primary sequence.

Clauses of Proviso

Clauses of proviso give a condition for the main clause. They take the subjunctive and are introduced by the following conjunctions:

dum	provided that
modo	provided that
dummodo	provided that

Rēx populō aurum dōnābit *dummodō* mīlitēs urbem capiant.	The king will give money to the *people provided that the soldiers capture the city.*

Exercises

3. Translate the following. Then identify the type of subordinate clause in each sentence.

   1. Populus timet nē avāritia rēgis regnum dēleat.

   _____

   2. Poēta timēbat nē avāritia regnum dēlēvisset.

   _____

   3. Rēx poētās dēterret quōminus librōs scrībant.

   _____

   4. Rēx mīlitēs nōn dēterrēbit quīn poētās interficiant.

   _____

   5. Rōmānī nōn dubitābant quīn imperium esset maximum bonōrum.

   _____

   _____

   6. Poēta rēgem ōrābant nē librī dēlērentur.

   _____

   7. Rēx librōs nōn dēlēbit modo mīlitēs poētās interficiant.

   _____

   8. Rēx poētās interficere vult ut populus esset librīs līber.

   _____

   9. Pōetae a rēge sīc interficiēbantur ut populus multum timēret.

   _____

   _____

10. Tam magna erat avāritia rēgis ut populus nunc sit populus servōrum.

_____

_____

4. Translate the following sentences.

1. Erat tam dēmēns is ut omnīs suās fortūnās aliēnīs servīs committeret?

_____

2. Vincat aliquandō cupiditās voluptāsque ratiōnem, dum modo illa praescriptiō moderātiōque teneātur.

_____

_____

_____

3. Sed iam, ut omnī mē invidiā līberem, pōnam in mediō sententiās philosophōrum dē natūrā deōrum.

_____

_____

_____

4. Sed cum mihi, patrēs conscriptī, et prō mē aliquid et in Antōnium multa dīcenda sint, alterum petō a vōbīs, ut mē prō mē dīcentem benignē, alterum ipse efficiam, ut contrā illum cum dīcam attentē audiātis.

_____

_____

_____

_____

_____

5. Tu istīs faucibus, istīs lateribus, ista gladiātōriā tōtīus corporis firmitāte tantum vīnī in Hippiae nuptiīs exhauserās ut tibi necesse esset in populī Rōmānī conspectū vomere postrīdiē.

_____

_____

_____

_____

_____

6. Cūr aut tam familiāris fuistī ut aurum commodārēs aut tam inimīca ut venēnum timērēs?

_____

_____

_____

7. An timēbant nē tot ūnum, valentēs imbecillum, alācrēs perterritum superāre nōn possent?

_____
_____
_____

8. Nec dubitārī dēbet quīn fuerint ante Homērum poētae.

_____
_____

9. Quam ob rem discēde atque hunc mihi timōrem ēripe; si est vērus, nē opprimar, sīn falsus, ut tandem aliquandō timēre dēsinam.

_____
_____
_____
_____

Vocabulary

dēmēns, -ntis	insane
fortūna, -ae, f.	fortune, wealth
aliēnus, -a, -um	belonging to another person
committo, committere	entrust
vincō, vincere	conquer
aliquandō	sometimes
cupiditās, -tātis, f.	desire
voluptās, -tātis, f.	pleasure
ratiō, -ōnis, f.	reasoning, rational thought
ille, illa, illud	(here) the following
praescriptiō, -ōnis, f.	precept, rule
moderātiō, -ōnis, f.	moderation, control
invidia, -ae, f.	ill will
līberō, līberāre	free
sententia, -ae, f.	thought, opinion
philosophus, -ī, m.	philosopher
patrēs cōnscriptī	senators
Antōnius, -ī, m.	Antonius
alter, -tra, -trum	one (of two)
benignē (adv.)	benevolently, in a friendly manner
efficiō, efficere	bring about, effect
attentē (adv.)	attentively
faucēs, -ium, f. pl.	throat

latus, lateris, n.	side, flank
gladiātōrius, -a, -um	of a gladiator
firmitās, -tātis, f.	strength
vīnum, -ī, n.	wine
Hippia, -ae, f.	Hippia (a woman's name)
nuptiae, -ārum, f. pl.	wedding
exhauriō, exhaurīre	drain, drink up
conspectus, -ūs, m.	sight, view
vomō, vomere	vomit
postrīdiē (adv.)	on the following day
cūr	why
aut . . . aut	either . . . or
familiāris, -e	friendly, intimate
commodō, commodāre	lend
inimīcus, -a, -um	enemy, hostile
venēnum, -ī, n.	poison
tot (indeclinable)	so many (here, so many men)
valēns, -ntis	strong, powerful
imbēcillus, -a, -um	weak
alacer, -cris, -cre	swift
perterritus, -a, -um	thoroughly terrified
superō, superāre	overcome
dēbeō, dēbēre	owe, ought (+ inf.)
quam ob rem	for which reason[2]
discēdo, discēdere	leave, depart
timor, -ōris, m.	fear
vērus, -a, -um	true, real
opprimō, opprimere	oppress
sīn	but if
falsus, -a, -um	false, unreal
ēripiō, ēripere	tear away, remove
tandem (adv.)	finally, at last
aliquandō	at some time, ever
timeō, timēre	fear
dēsinō, dēsinere	cease (+ inf.)

---

[2] Referring to something mentioned earlier.

Conditional Sentences

Conditional sentences are composed of two clauses:

If he works, he is happy

"If he works," the subordinate clause, gives the *condition* for which the main clause will be true.

Latin grammars traditionally refer to the "if" clause of a conditional sentence as the *protasis* and the main clause as the *apodosis*.

There are generally three kinds of conditional sentence:

Simple conditions

Future conditions

Contrary-to-fact conditions

These categories differ according to the tense and mood of the verb they employ in the protasis and the apodosis.

The subordinating conjunction "if" in Latin is **sī**. Its negative is **nisī**. The main clause is negated normally, with **nōn**.

SIMPLE CONDITIONS

Simple conditions take a present or past tense of the indicative in both the protasis and apodosis. They should be translated accordingly.

Sī labōrat, miser est.	If he works, he is wretched.
Nisī labōrābat, fēlix erat.	If he was not working, he was happy.

FUTURE CONDITIONS

There are three kinds of future conditions. *Future-more-vivid conditions* take the future indicative in both the protasis and the apodosis.

Sī mīlitēs urbem *capient*, poētae *canent*.

For convenience in English, the future indicative in the "if" clause "if the soldiers will capture" is usually translated as a present:

If the soldiers *capture* the city, the poets *will sing*.

Sometimes in this type of condition the future perfect is used instead of the ordinary future indicative:

Sī mīlitēs urbem *cēperint*, poētae *canent*.

Although in Latin this is felt to be more emphatic,[3] the English translation remains the same:

> If the soldiers *capture* the city, the poets *will sing*.

Future-less-vivid conditions take the present subjunctive in both the protasis and the apodosis. In Latin these sentences are felt to imagine the situation less definitely or "vividly" than the "more vivid" examples.

> **Sī mīlitēs urbem *capiant*, poētae *canant*.**

Often these sentences are translated using "should" for the "if" clause and "would" for the main clause:

> If the soldiers *should capture* the city, the poets *would sing*.

Rēgīna miser sit nisī poēta canat.	The queen would be miserable if the poet should not sing.

Occasionally a sentence will take the future indicative in one clause and the present subjunctive in the other. Such sentences are known as mixed future conditions.

CONTRARY-TO-FACT CONDITIONS

Contrary-to-fact conditions refer to something unreal. (They are sometimes known as *unreal conditions*.) There are three kinds.

Present contrary-to-fact conditions refer to what is unreal in present time. They take the imperfect subjunctive in both the protasis and the apodosis:

Sī mīlitēs urbem *caperent*, poētae *canerent*.	If the soldiers *were capturing* the city, the poets *would be singing*.

We know from both the Latin and the English translation that these things are not happening now.

If the protasis is negated, it *is* happening:

Nisī ad mare *ambulārem*, *labōrārem*.	If I *were not walking* to the sea, I *would be working*.

From this it is clear that I *am* walking to the sea and therefore that I am *not* working.

Past contrary-to-fact conditions refer to what is unreal in past time. They take the pluperfect subjunctive in both the protasis and the apodosis:

Sī mīlitēs urbem *cēpissent*, poētae *cecinissent*.	If the soldiers *had captured* the city, the poets *would have sung*.

---

[3] Some grammars refer to this type as *future most vivid* or *future more vivid with emphatic protasis*.

We know from both the Latin and the English translation that these things did not happen then in the past.

Labōrāvissēmus nisī ad mare ambulāvissēmus.	We *would have worked* if we *had not walked* to the sea.

Mixed contrary-to-fact conditions refer to something that is unreal in the present because of something unreal in the past. They take the pluperfect subjunctive in the "if" clause and the imperfect subjunctive in the main clause:

Sī mīlitēs urbem *cēpissent*, poēta *canerent.*	If the soldiers *had captured* the city, the poets *would be singing*.

We know from both the Latin and the English translation that the soldiers did not capture the city in the past and that therefore the poets are not singing now.

Exercises

5. Translate the following conditional sentences. Then identify what type they are.

1. Sī rēx dēmēns regnum dēlēbit, poētae Rōmam fugient.

_____

_____

2. Nisī rēx dēmēns regnum dēlēvisset, poētae Rōmam nōn fūgissent.

_____

_____

3. Nisī fīlius fidem servet, pater sit miserrimus.

_____

_____

4. Nisī fīlius fidem servāret, pater esset miserrimus.

_____

_____

5. Nisi illō tempore fīlius fidem servāvisset, pater nunc esset miserrimus.

_____

_____

6. Sī in urbe multī poēta ambulant, et rēgīnae et populō pācem dōnant.

_____

_____

7. Sī rēx poētās interficiat, populus timeat.

_____

_____

8. Sī rēx dēmēns poētās interfēcerit, populus multum timēbit.

_____

_____

_____

9. Sī ā rēge dēmentī poēta magnus interfectus esset, pācem rēgīna dēlēvisset.

_____

_____

_____

10. Sī poēta magnus a rēge interficiētur, rēgīna pācem dēlēbit.

_____

_____

_____

6. Translate the following sentences.

1. Memoriam quoque ipsam cum vōce perdidissēmus sī tam in nostrā potestāte esset oblīvīscī quan tacēre.

_____

_____

_____

2. Multa ioca solent esse in epistulīs quae, prōlata sī sint, inepta videantur.

_____

_____

_____

3. Sī tē parentēs timērent neque eōs ulla ratiōne plācāre possēs, ab eōrum oculīs aliquō concēderēs.

_____

_____

_____

4. Quod sī invenīrētur aliqua cīvitās in quā nēmō peccāret, supervacuus esset inter innocentēs ōrātor sīcut inter sānōs medicus.

_____

_____

_____

5. Sed quid oppōnās tandem sī negem mē umquam ad tē istās litterās mīsisse?

_____

_____

_____

6. Diēs iam mē dēficiat sī quae dīcī in eam sententiam possunt cōner exprōmere.

_____

_____

_____

Vocabulary

memoria, -ae, f.	memory
quoque	also, in the same way
vox, vōcis, f.	voice
perdō, perdere, perdidī, perditus	lose, destroy
oblīvīscor, oblīvīscī, oblītus sum	forget
taceō, tacēre	be silent
iocum, ī, n.	joke
epistula, -ae, f.	letter
prōferō	bring forward, expose
video	(in passive) seem
ineptus, -a, -um	foolish
parēns, parentis, m./f.	parent
ratiō, -ōnis, f.	reasoning, way
plācō, plācāre	please
oculus, -ī, m.	eye
aliquō (adv.)	to some other place
concēdō, concēdere	withdraw
quod sī	but if
inveniō, invenīre	to find
cīvitās, -tātis, f.	citizenry, state
nēmō, nēminis	nobody
peccō, peccāre	commit an offense, sin
supervacuus, -a, -um	completely unnecessary
innocēns, -ntis	innocent
ōrātor, -ōris, m.	orator, lawyer
sīcut	just as
sānus, -a, -um	healthy, well
medicus, -ī, m.	doctor
oppōnō, oppōnere	oppose, say in opposition
tandem (adv.)	really, after all
negō, negāre	deny
umquam (adv.)	ever
litterae, -ārum, f. pl.	letter
mittō, mittere, mīsī, missus	send
dēficiō, dēficere	be lacking, run out
sententia, -ae, f.	thought, opinion

cōnor, cōnārī, cōnātus sum	try, attempt (+ inf.)
exprōmō, exprōmere	bring out, reveal, express

Relative Clauses with the Subjunctive

Ordinary relative clauses that take the indicative provide factual information about their antecedent. There are, however, a variety of relative clauses that take the subjunctive to express more complex meanings.

RELATIVE CLAUSE OF CHARACTERISTIC

A relative clause of characteristic gives generalizing or defining information about its antecedent.

Is est quī mortem timeat.	He is (the sort of person) who fears death.

This does not mean merely that he fears death, but that his fear of death is a natural part or result of his character.

Amō nihil quod puerīs noceat.	I love nothing (of the sort) which harms children.

Relative clauses of characteristic are often found with such general expressions as

Is est quī	He is (the sort) who
Sunt quī	There are those (of the sort) who
Nemō est quī	There is no one (of the sort) who
Nihil est quod	There is nothing (of the sort) which

However, they may just as often have specific antecedents:

Cicero erat quī litterās amāret.	Cicero was (the sort of person) who loved letters.

Other relative clauses that take the subjunctive correspond more closely to some of the subordinate clauses described above.

RELATIVE CLAUSE OF PURPOSE

A relative clause with the subjunctive, often after a verb of motion or action, can express purpose:

Rēx ad urbem mīlitēs mittet *quī poētās interficiant.*	The king will send soldiers to the city *in order that they may kill* the poets.

It is easier to translate these simply as purpose clauses.

Sometimes, if a place is indicated, the adverb **ubi** may be used as the relative:

Rēx ad urbem mīlitēs mittet *ubi poētās interficiant.*	The king will send soldiers to the city *in order that **there** they may kill* the poets.

Ubi is a relative adverb.

Sometimes a relative clause of purpose will be introduced by **quō** and contain a comparative adverb:

Rēx urbem capiet *quō facilius poētās interficiat.*	The king will capture the city *in order that **by this**[4] he may kill the poets more easily.*

RELATIVE CLAUSE OF RESULT

A relative clause with the subjunctive, often with an intensifier, can express result:

Rēx erat tam dēmēns *quī urbem dēlēret.*	The king was so insane *that he destroyed the city.*

It is easier to translate these simply as result clauses.

RELATIVE CLAUSE OF CAUSE

A relative clause with the subjunctive can express cause. Sometimes (but not always) the relative pronoun will be preceded by **ut**, **utpote**, or **quippe**.

Rēx *quippe quī dēmēns esset* urbem dēlēvit.	The king, *because he was insane,* destroyed the city.
Cicerō ut quī litterās amāret lībertātem populī dēfendit.	Cicero, *in as much as he loved letters,* defended the liberty of the people.

Exercises

7. Translate the following sentences.

   1. Ad urbem vēnērunt poētae quī librōs scrīberent.

   _____

   2. Tam caecī erant poētae quī perīculum nōn vidērent.

   _____

   3. Sunt quī pecūniam plūs quam lībertātem ament.

   _____

---

[4] The antecedent of **quō** here is the whole action of the main clause, i.e., the capturing of the city "by which" the main clause may be accomplished.

4. Rēx ut quī pecūniam plūs quam lībertātem amāret bellum parābat.

_____

_____

5. Mīlitēs petēbant id quod amārent plūs quam pecūniam.

_____

_____

8. Translate the following sentences.

1. Quid est quod tū nōn audeās?

_____

_____

2. Tum dēnique interficiēre cum iam nēmō tam improbus, tam perditus, tam tuī similis invenīrī poterit quī id nōn iure factum esse fateātur. Quamdiu quisquam erit quī dēfendere audeat, vīvēs.

_____

_____

_____

_____

3. Quid est enim, Catilīna, quod tē iam in hāc urbe dēlectāre possit, in quā nēmō est, extra istam coniūrātiōnem perditōrum hominum quī tē nōn metuat, nēmo quī nōn ōderit?

_____

_____

_____

_____

_____

4. Mittitur Dēcidius cum paucīs quī locī nātūram perspiciat.

_____

5. Accipite nunc, quaesō, nōn ea quae ipse in sē atque in domesticum decus impūrē et intemperanter, sed quae in nōs fortūnāsque, id est in ūniversam rem pūblicam, impiē ac nefāriē fēcerit.

_____

_____

_____

_____

6. Quid enim mē interpōnerem audāciae tuae quam neque auctōritās huius ordinis neque existimātiō populī Rōmānī neque lēgēs ullae possent coercēre?

_____

_____

_____

Vocabulary

audeō, audēre, ausum sum	dare
dēnique (adv.)	finally
interficiō, interficere	kill
nēmō, nēminis	nobody
improbus, -a, -um	base, depraved
similis, -e	similar
inveniō, invenīre	find
iūre	rightly
fateor, fatērī, fassus sum	confess
quamdiū (adv.)	as long as
dēfendō, dēfendere	defend
vīvō, vīvere	live
enim	indeed
Catilīna, -ae, m.	Catiline
dēlectō, dēlectāre	please, delight
coniūrātiō, -ōnis, f.	conspiracy
metuō, mctucrc	fear
ōdī, ōdisse	hate
Dēcidius, -ī, m.	Decidius
paucī, -ae, -a	few
locus, -ī, m.	place
nātūra, -ae, f.	nature
perspiciō, perspicere	look over, inspect
accipiō, accipere	receive, hear
quaesō	please
domesticus, -a, -um	domestic, private
decus, decoris, n.	honor
impūrē (adv.)	impurely, basely
intemperanter (adv.)	intemperately
ūniversis, -a, -um	whole, entire
impiē (adv.)	impiously
nefāriē (adv.)	monstrously

quid	(here) why?
interpōnō, interpōnere	place as an obstacle, interpose
audācia, -ae, f.	audacity
auctōritās, -tātis, f.	authority
ordō, ordinis	order, body of men
existimātiō, -ōnis, f.	judgment, opinion
lex, lēgis, f.	law
coerceō, coercēre	restrain, confine

Participles Revisited

Participles, as stated before, are verbal adjectives. As such, they modify nouns.

Mīlitēs canentēs templum dēlēvērunt.   The *singing* soldiers destroyed the
temple.

Here the participle functions simply as an adjective, giving us information about the soldiers.

We could also translate this participle more as an adverb, telling us something about *how* the soldiers performed the action of the main verb:

Singing, the soldiers destroyed the temple.

Although the example above is quite simple, participles can often extend this more adverbial usage to do the work of entire subordinate clauses. For example, they may have temporal force, simply correlating their action in time with the main verb:

Mīlitēs urbem capientēs **templum**   *When they were capturing the city*, they
dēlēverunt.   destroyed the temple.

They may have causal force, explaining the action of the main verb:

Mīlitēs urbem capientēs **gaudēbant.**   *Because they were capturing the city*, the
soldiers were happy.

The presence of the word **tamen** may show that a participle is being used concessively:

Mīlitēs urbem capientēs **templum**   *Although they were capturing the city*,
tamen nōn dēlēvērunt.   nevertheless the soldiers did not
destroy the temple.

A participle can act as the protasis of a conditional sentence. When it does, the main verb will indicate what type of conditional sentence it is.

***Mīlitēs urbem capientēs* templum dēlēbunt.**	*If the soldiers capture the city*, they will destroy the temple.

The future indicative **dēlēbunt** indicates a future-more-vivid conditional sentence.

***Mīlitēs urbem capientēs* templum dēlērent.**	*If the soldiers were capturing the city*, they would be destroying the temple.

The imperfect subjunctive **dēlērent** indicates a present contrary-to-fact conditional sentence.

Urbs capta dēlēta esset.	If it had been captured, the city would have been destroyed.

The pluperfect subjunctive **dēlēta esset** indicates a past contrary-to-fact conditional sentence.

Although in an isolated sentence like this such different possibilities may seem arbitrary, the actual context of written Latin will make it easier to see how best to translate such hard-working participles.

Exercise

9. Translate the following using as many of the above senses of the participle as is reasonably possible.

1. Pōetae canentī pecūniam rēx dōnābit.

    _____

2. Pōetae canentī rēx tamen pecūniam nōn dedit.

    _____

3. Poētae canentī rēx pecūniam dōnāret.

    _____

4. Poētīs ā mīlitibus captīs rēx pecūniam nōn dedisset.

    _____

5. Rēx poētīs a mīlitibus captīs pecūniam dāns ā rēgīnā amētur.

    _____

Ablative Absolute

A participle together with the noun it modifies, both in the ablative case, form a construction known as the ablative absolute. Together they represent another set of circumstances that accompanies the main clause in the sentence.

***Mīlitibus urbem capientibus* rēx timēbat.**	*With the soldiers capturing* the city, the king was afraid.

Although it lacks a subordinating conjunction, the ablative absolute is like a subordinate clause in that it cannot stand on its own. However, its subject must be different from that of the main clause.[5]

Litterīs recitātīs **rēx gemuit.**	With the letter having been read, the king groaned.

Like other participles, the participle in an ablative absolute may have different meanings based on context:

Because the letter had been read, the king groaned.

When the letter had been read, the king groaned.

Although the letter had been read, the king groaned.

Relative time applies. Whatever the force of **recitātīs**, its perfect tense shows time prior to that of the main verb **gemuit**.

Rēge moriente,[6] **rēgīna tamen discēssit.**	Although the king was dying, the queen departed.

The present participle shows time simultaneous with the perfect **discēssit**. **Tamen** indicates that the ablative absolute should be translated as a concessive clause.

Poētīs *interfectīs* **rēx tamen timēbat.**	Although the poets *had been killed*, nevertheless, the king was afraid.

The perfect participle shows time prior to the main verb.

An ablative absolute can function as the protasis of a conditional sentence:

Mīlitibus captīs, rēx nōn timuisset.	If the soldiers had been captured, the king would not have been afraid.

The pluperfect subjunctive **timuisset** indicates that the sentence is a past contrary-to-fact conditional sentence.

Sometimes an ablative absolute will not contain a participle, but another noun or adjective in the ablative that acts as a predicate:

Poētā rēge fēlix erit rēgīna.	If the poet is king, the queen will be happy.

Here **rēge** is predicate to the subject. The verb **sum**, " to be," has no participle that could be used here, but the sense may be supplied.

Exercises

10. Translate the following.

1. Servīs fugientibus, mīlitēs urbem dēlēvērunt.

_____

_____

---

[5] "Absolute" in this sense means free from connection to the main clause.
[6] When the singular of the present participle is used in an ablative absolute, it takes the ending **-ē** instead of **-ī**.

2. Servīs fugientibus, mīlitēs urbem dēlēbunt.

_____

3. Servīs fugientibus mīlitēs urbem dēlērent.

_____

4. Urbe ā mīlitibus dēlētā imperātor clāmāvit sē esse rēgem.

_____

5. Urbe ā mīlitibus dēlētā imperātor sē esse rēgem clāmāvisset.

_____

6. Urbe ā mīlitibus dēlētā imperātor sē esse rēgem clāmābit.

_____

7. Imperātōre sē esse rēgem clāmante servī ex urbe fugiēbant.

_____

8. Imperātōre rēge servī multum timēbunt.

_____

9. Imperātōre rēge servī multum timuissent.

_____

10. Imperātōre sē esse rēgem urbis clāmante mīlitēs tamen discessērunt.

_____

_____

11.   Translate the following sentences.

1. Itaque vastātīs omnibus eōrum agrīs, vīcīs aedificiīsque incēnsīs, Caesar exercitum redūxit et in hīherniīs collocāvit.

_____

_____

_____

2. Exiguā parte aestātis reliquā Caesar tamen in Britanniam proficīscī contendit.

_____

_____

3. Et sīcut vetus aetās vīdit quid ultimum in libertāte esset, ita nōs quid in servitūte, ademptō per inquīsītiōnēs etiam loquendī audiendīque commerciō.

_____

_____

_____

Vocabulary

itaque (adv.)	and so
vastō, vastāre	lay waste, destroy
agrum, -ī, n.	field
vīcus, -ī, m.	village
aedificium, -ī, n.	building
incendō, incendere	burn
Caesar, Caesaris, m.	Caesar
exercitus, -ūs, m.	army
redūcō, redūcere	lead back
hīberna, -ōrum, n. pl.	winter camp
collocō, collocāre	put in place, settle, locate
exiguus, -a, -um	small
aestās, -tātis, f.	summer
relīquus, -a, -um	remaining, left over
Britannia, -ae, f.	Britain
proficīscor, proficīscī, profectus sum	set forth
contendō, contendere	make an effort, hurry
vetus, veteris	old
aetās, -tātis, f.	time, age
ultimus, -a, -um	furthest, most extreme
lībertās, -tātis, f.	liberty
servitus, -tūtis, f.	slavery
adimō, adimere, adēmī, ademptus	remove, take away
inquīsītiō, -ōnis, f.	trial
loquor, loquī, locūtus sum	speak
commercium, -ī, n.	exchange, commerce

Indirect Statement

An indirect statement is the reporting of another statement, originally "direct."

Direct: The poets are working in the field.

Indirect: He says that the poets are working in the field.

English uses the conjunction "that" to make a subordinate clause of the original direct statement.

Latin does not express indirect statement by subordinate clause. Instead, it uses a *subject accusative* and *infinitive* construction. That is, the subject of the statement given in indirect form will be put into the accusative case and the verb in the infinitive:

Dīcit *poētās* in agrō *labōrāre.*	He says that the poets are working in the field.

The English word "that" must be supplied in the translation, though the Latin does not have it.

Any word signifying thought, speech, feeling, rumor, etc. can initiate an indirect statement:

***Rūmor erat* poētās in agrō labōrāre.**	*There was a rumor that* the poets were working in the field.

Remember that, like participles, infinitives in Latin show only three tenses: present, perfect, and future. Also like participles, infinitives in an indirect statement must be translated according to the rules of relative time.

The present infinitive shows time simultaneous with that of the main verb:

Dīcēbat* poētās in agrō *labōrāre.	He said that the poets *were working* in the field.

Here the present infinitive **labōrāre** shows time simultaneous with the main verb **dīcēbat** in the imperfect tense and so is translated "were working."

Dīcet* poētās in agrō *labōrāre.	He will say that the poets *are working.*[7]

The perfect infinitive shows time prior to that of the main verb:

Dīcit* poētās in agrō *labōrāvisse.	He says that the poets *worked* in the field.
Dīcēbat* poētās in agrō *labōrāvisse.	He said that the poets *had worked* in the fields.
Dīcet* poētās in agrō *labōrāvisse.	He will say that the poets *have worked* in the fields.

The future infinitive shows time subsequent to that of the main verb:

Dīcit* poētās in agrō *labōrātūrōs esse.	He says that the poets *will work* in the field.
Dīcēbat* poētās in agrō *labōrātūrōs esse.	He said that the poets *would work* in the field.
Dīcet* poētās in agrō *labōrātūrōs esse.	He will say that the poets *will work* in the field.

---

[7] Here the English says "are working." It means they will be working at the same time as he says it.

Note that the form of the future infinitive **labōrātūrōs esse** must agree in gender, number, and case with the subject accusative **poētās**, which is masculine accusative plural.

A subject of different gender and number would require a different form:

Dīcit *fēminām* in agrō *labōrātūram* esse.   He says that the woman will work in the field.

Here **labōrātūram** agrees with the feminine noun **fēminam**.

This consideration also applies to the perfect passive infinitive:

Dīcit urbem capt*am* esse.   He says that the city was captured.

Here **captam** must agree with the feminine **urbem**.

Exercises

12.   Translate the following. Pay particular attention to the relative time of the infinitive and the main verb.

1. Putāmus rēgīnam esse miseram.

   _____

2. Putāmus rēgīnam miseram fuisse.

   _____

3. Putāmus rēgīnam cum nōbīs nōn locūtūram esse.

   _____

4. Putat mātrēs mīlitum mortuōrum ad mare ambulāre.

   _____

5. Putābat mātrēs mīlitum mortuōrum ad mare ambulāvisse.

   _____

6. Rūmor est mātrēs mīlitum mortuōrum ad mare ambulātūrās esse.

   _____

7. Rūmor erat matrēs mīlitum mortuōrum ad mare ambulātūrās esse.

   _____

8. Dīcit animālia ā puerīs spectārī.

   _____

9. Dīcit animālia ā puerīs spectāta esse.

   _____

10. Dīxit animālia a puerīs spectārī.

11. Dīxit animālia a puerīs spectāta esse.

   _____

12. Dīxit puerōs animālia spectatūrōs esse.

13. Dīxit animālia puerōs spectatūra esse.

14. Nēmō crēdit rēgem poētās interfectūrum esse.

15. Quis crēdat rēgem pōetās interfēcisse?

13. Translate the following sentences.

1. Crēdibile est igitur tantum facinus nullam ob causam esse commissum?

2. Iam intelligēs multō mē vigilāre ācrius ad salūtem quam tē ad perniciem reī pūblicae.

3. Dolēbam, dolēbam, patrēs conscriptī, rem pūblicam vestrīs quondam meīsque cōnsiliīs conservātam brevī tempore esse peritūram.

4. Sunt enim philosophī et fuērunt quī omnīnō nullam habēre censērent rērum hūmanārum prōcūrātiōnem deōs. Quōrum sī vēra sententia est, quae potest esse pietās, quae sanctitās, quae religiō?... Sunt autem aliī philosophī, et hī quidem magnī atque nōbilēs, quī deōrum mente atque ratiōne omnem mundum administrārī et rēgī censeant...

5. Homo disertus nōn intelligit eum quem contrā dīcit laudārī ā sē; eōs apud quōs dīcit vituperārī.

Vocabulary

crēdibilis, -e	believable
igitur (adv.)	therefore, then
facinus, facinoris, n.	crime
committō, committere	commit
intelligō, intelligere	understand, discern
vigilō, vigilāre	keep watch, stay awake
ācer, -cris, -cre	sharp, keen
salūs, -ūtis, f.	health, safety
perniciēs, -ēī, f.	destruction, ruin
doleō, dolēre	grieve, be in pain
patrēs conscriptī	senators
cōnsilium, -ī, n.	advice, planning
quondam (adv.)	at some time in the past, formerly
conservō, conservāre	save, preserve
brevis, -e	brief, short
pereō, perīre, periī, peritūrus[8]	perish, die
enim	for
philosophus, -ī, m.	philosopher
omnīnō (adv.)	entirely
cēnseō, cēnsēre	judge
hūmānus, -a, -um	of humans
prōcūrātiō, -ōnis, f.	concern, care, responsibility
vērus, -a, -um	true
sententia, -ae, f.	opinion, thought
pietās, -tātis, f.	devotion, loyalty
sanctitās, -tātis, f.	moral purity, sanctity
religiō, -ōnis, f.	religion
autem	moreover
quidem	indeed
nōbilis, -e	noble
rātiō, -ōnis, f.	reason, reckoning
mundus, -ī, m.	world
administrō, administrāre	conduct, manage, administer
regō, regere	rule

---

[8] The fourth principal part given here is the future active participle.

disertus, -a, -um	learned, clever
intelligō, intelligere	understand
laudō, laudāre	praise
vituperō, vituperāre	criticize

Indirect Question

Questions in Latin are often introduced by interrogative words or expressions such as the following:

quis, quid	who, what
quō modō	how
quam ob rem	why
cūr	why
quandō	when
ubi	where
unde	from where

| **Cūr clāmāvit?** | Why did he shout? |
| **Unde venis?** | Where are you coming from? |

An indirect question, as the name suggests, is a question reported in indirect form. Latin expresses indirect questions as subordinate clauses. The interrogative word of the original question acts as a subordinating conjunction, and the verb of the original direct question goes into the subjunctive according to the rules of sequence.

| **Quis hoc dīcit?** | Who says this? |
| **Rogat *quis hoc dīcat.*** | He asks *who says this.* |

The original direct question is now subordinated to the main verb **rogat.**

The present subjunctive expresses time simultaneous with the main verb in primary sequence. (It stands for an original present indicative.)

| **Rogat quis hoc *dīxerit.*** | He asks who *said* that. |

The perfect subjunctive expresses time prior to the main verb in secondary sequence.

Because there is no future subjunctive, to express time subsequent to the main verb in an indirect question, Latin uses the subjunctive of the active periphrastic (see p. 63).

| **Rogat quis hoc *dictūrus sit.*** | He asks who *is going to (will) say* this. |

Here the present subjunctive of the active periphrastic is used in primary sequence.

In secondary sequence, the imperfect subjunctive expresses time simultaneous with the main verb:

| **Rogāvit quis hoc *dīceret.*** | He asked who *was saying* this. |

The pluperfect subjunctive expresses time prior to that of the main verb:

Rogāvit quis hoc *dīxisset.*   He asked who *had said* this.

To express time subsequent to the main verb in secondary sequence, the imperfect subjunctive of the active periphrastic is used:

Rogāvit quis hoc *dictūrus esset.*   He asked who *was going to say* this.

Direct questions may not always be introduced by an interrogative word:

Labōrat?   Does he work?

In such cases Latin may use the word **utrum** or the interrogative enclitic **-ne**.

Rogō labōretne.
Rogō utrum labōret.
I ask whether he works.

Exercises

14.   Translate the following.

  1. Mīrāmur cūr clāmēs.

  _____

  2. Mirābāmur cūr clāmāvissētis.

  _____

  3. Nesciō cūr clāmāverint.

  _____

  4. Scītis quibus rēx aurum dōnatūrus sit?

  _____

  5. Sciēbātis cui rēx aurum dōnātūrus esset.

  _____

  6. Mihi dīcere nōluit quō modō mīlitēs urbem dēlēvissent.

  _____

  7. Nēmō mihi dīcere potest quam ob rem urbs a mīlitibus dēleātur.

  _____

  8. Dīc mihi ā quō interfectus sit rēx.

  _____

  9. Rogāvit cūr non amārēmur.

  10. Quis rogāvit cūr nōn amātī essēmus?

  _____

15.   Translate the following sentences.

  1. Ego quid ille et contrā ille quid ego sentīrem et spectārem vidēbat.

  _____

2. Ille quid ego et contrā ego quid ille sentīret et spectāret vidēbam.

_____

3. Quae fuit enim causa quam ob rem istī mulierī venēnum dare vellet
Caelius?... Sed tamem venēnum unde fuerit, quem ad modum
parātum sit nōn dīcitur.

_____
_____
_____
_____
_____

4. Itaque hodiē perficiam ut intelligat quantum ā mē beneficium tum
accēperit.

_____
_____

5. Et sīcut vetus aetās vīdit quid ultimum in libertāte esset, ita nōs quid
in servitūte, ademptō per inquīsītiōnēs etiam loquendī audiendīque
commerciō.

_____
_____
_____
_____
_____

Vocabulary

contrā (adv.)	on the other side, on the other hand
sentiō, sentīre	feel, think
spectō, spectāre	look at, watch for
iste, ista, istud	that (often with contempt)
mulier, mulieris, f.	woman
venēnum, -ī, n.	poison
unde	from where?
quem ad modum	in what manner?
itaque	and so, in this manner
hodiē (adv.)	today
perficiō, perficere	accomplish, effect
intelligō, intelligere	understand
quantus, -a, -um	how great?
beneficium, -ī, n.	benefit, favor
tum	at that time
accipiō, accipere	receive, take, accept

vetus, veteris	old
aetās, -tātis, f.	time, age
ultimus, -a, -um	furthest, most extreme
lībertās, -tātis, f.	liberty
servitus, -tūtis, f.	slavery
adimō, adimere, adēmī, ademptus	remove, take away
inquīsītiō, -ōnis, f.	trial
loquor, loquī, locūtus sum	speak
commercium, -ī, n.	exchange, commerce

Exercise

16. (Advanced reading) Translate the following passage and do the exercise at the end.

In this opening passage from his speech Pro Caelio, Cicero comments on the unusual nature of a trial that is taking place on a public holiday, when the courts would normally be closed.

Sī quis, iūdicēs, forte nunc *adsit* ignārus lēgum, iūdiciōrum, consuētūdinis nostrae, *mirētur* profectō quae *sit* tanta atrōcitās huius causae *quod diēbus festīs lūdīsque* pūblicīs, *omnibus forensibus negōtiīs intermissīs,* ūnum hoc iūdicium *exerceātur,* nec dubitet quīn tantī facinoris reus *arguātur* ut eo neglectō cīvitās stāre nōn *possit*;

(The passage continues on p. 160.)

Vocabulary

iūdex, iūdicis, m.	judge
forte	perhaps
adsum, adesse	be present
ignārus, -a, -um	ignorant, without knowledge (+ gen.)
lex, lēgis, f.	law
iūdicium, ī, n.	trial
consuētūdō, -tūdinis, f.	habit, practice
mīror, mīrārī, mīrātus sum	wonder
profectō	undoubtedly
tantus, -a, -um	so great
atrōcitās, -tātis, f.	terribleness
causa, -ae, f.	case
diēs festus	holiday

lūdus, ī, m.	game, entertainment
pūblicus, -a, -um	public
forensis, -e	pertaining to the law courts
negōtium, -ī, n.	business
intermittō, intermittere, intermīsī, intermissus	interrupt, suspend
exerceō, exercēre	exercise, practice, conduct
facinus, facinoris, n.	crime
reus, -ī, m.	defendant
arguō, arguere	accuse
neglegō, neglegere, neglēxī, neglēctus	neglect
cīvitās, -tātis, f.	citizenry, state
stō, stāre	stand

Exercise

1. Identify and explain the tense and mood of **adsit**.

   _____
   _____
   _____

2. Identify and explain the tense and mood of **mīrētur**.

   _____
   _____
   _____
   _____

3. Identify and explain the tense and mood of **sit**.

   _____
   _____
   _____

4. Explain the case of **diēbus festīs**.

   _____
   _____
   _____

5. What kind of construction is **omnibus forensibus negōtiīs intermissīs**?

   _____
   _____
   _____

6. Identify and explain the tense and mood of **arguātur**.

   _____
   _____

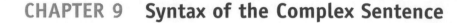

7. Identify and explain the tense and mood of **possit**.

_____
_____
_____

Subordinate Clauses in Indirect Statement

The section above on indirect statement deals with the indirect expression of simple sentences consisting of one independent clause. Such a clause, in indirect form, puts its subject in the accusative case and its verb in the infinitive.

When complex sentences are put into indirect statement, the main and subordinate clauses behave differently. The main clause, as explained above, takes the subject accusative and infinitive construction. Subordinate clauses generally put their verbs into the subjunctive according to the rules of sequence and relative time.

Quamquam urbs dēletur poētae tamen manent.	Although the city is being destroyed, nevertheless the poets are remaining.
Dīcit quamquam urbs _dēleātur_, poētās tamen manēre.	He says that although the city _is being destroyed_, nevertheless the poets are remaining.

The present subjunctive stands for an original present indicative in primary sequence, expressing time simultaneous with the main verb.

Sometimes the subject and infinitive may enclose the subordinate clause:

> **Dīcit poētās quamquam urbs dēleātur manēre tamen.**

In secondary sequence, only the subordinate clause is affected.

Dīxit quamquam urbs _dēlērētur_, poētās tamen manēre.	He said that although the city was being destroyed, nevertheless the poets were remaining.

Now the imperfect subjunctive stands for the original present indicative in secondary sequence, expressing time simultaneous with the main verb.

All the considerations of relative time will apply in translation:

Dīxit quamquam urbs _dēlēta esset_, poētās tamen _mānsūrōs esse._	He said that although the city _had been destroyed_, nevertheless the poets _would remain_.

Here the pluperfect subjunctive **dēlēta esset** represents time prior to the main verb **dīxit** in a subordinate clause in indirect statement in secondary sequence. The future infinitive represents time subsequent to that of the main verb.

Subordinate clauses that normally take the subjunctive, not surprisingly, will still take the subjunctive in indirect statement:

Cum urbs dēleātur, poētae fugient.

Because the city is being destroyed, the poets will flee.

Dīcit cum urbs dēleātur, poētas fugitūrōs esse.

He says that because the city is being destroyed, the poets will flee.

Relative Clauses in Indirect Statement

Relative clauses in indirect statement also take the subjunctive:

Rēx quī urbem dēlēvit dēmēns est.

The king who destroyed the city is insane.

Dīcit rēgem quī urbem *dēlēverit* dēmentem esse.

He says that the king who destroyed the city is insane.

Here the perfect subjunctive **dēlēverit** represents time prior to the main verb **dīcit** in a relative clause in indirect statement in primary sequence.

Dīcēbat rēgem quī urbem dēlēvisset dēmentem esse.

He said that the king who had destroyed the town was mad.

Here the pluperfect subjunctive **dēlēvisset** represents time prior to the main verb **dīcēbat** in a relative clause in indirect statement in secondary structure.

Sometimes, however, relative clauses inside an indirect statement will take the indicative. This usually means that the writer of the sentence is giving this information, adding it to the original direct statement:

Dīcit rēgem quī urbem *dēlēvit* dēmentem esse.

He says that the king who *(I am actually telling you) destroyed* the city is mad.

Although this translation is somewhat exaggerated, it is meant to show the difference between the indicative and subjunctive. The indicative tells you that the relative clause has been inserted by the writer, or at least that he confirms the truth of its contents.

Exercises

17. Translate the following sentences.

1. Quod dē lībertāte clāmant rēx poētās interficit.

   _____

   _____

2. Rēgīna dīcit rēgem quod dē lībertāte clāment poētās interficere.

   _____

   _____

   _____

3. Rēgīna dīcēbat rēgem quod dē lībertāte clāmārent poētās interficere.

_____

_____

4. Rēgīna dīcit rēgem quod dē lībertāte clāmāverint poētās interfēcisse.

_____

_____

5. Rēgīna dīcit rēgem poētās quod dē lībertāte clāmāverint interfectūrum esse.

_____

_____

6. Rēgīna dīcēbat rēgem poētās quod dē lībertāte clāmārent interfēcisse.

_____

_____

7. Rēgīna dīcēbat rēgem poētās quod dē lībertāte clāmāvissent interfectūrum esse.

_____

_____

8. Rēgīna dīcēbat rēgem quī populum timēret poētās quod dē lībertāte clāmāvissent interfēcisse.

_____

_____

_____

9. Rēgīna dīcēbat rēgem quī populum timēret poētās quod dē lībertāte clāmārent interfectūrum esse.

_____

_____

_____

_____

18. (Advanced reading; continued from p. 156) Translate the following passage and do the exercise at the end.

Īdem cum audiat esse lēgem quae dē sēditiōsīs conscelerātīsque cīvibus quī armātī senātum obsēderint, magistrātibus vim attulerint, rem pūblicam oppugnāverint, cōtīdiē quaerī iubeat, lēgem nōn improbet, crīmen quod versētur in iudiciō requīrat; cum audiat nullum facinus, nullam audāciam, nullam vim in iūdicium vocārī, sed adulescentem illustrī ingeniō, industriā, grātiā accūsārī ab ēius fīliō quem ipse in iūdicium et vocet et vocāverit, oppugnārī autem opibus meretrīcius, illīus pietātem nōn reprehendat, muliebrem libīdinem comprimendam putet, vōs labōriōsōs existimet, quibus otiōsīs nē in commūnī quidem ōtiō liceat esse.

(This passage continues on p. 165.)

_____

_____

_____

_____

_____

_____

_____

_____

_____

_____

_____

_____

_____

_____

_____

_____

_____

Vocabulary

lex, lēgis, f.	law
sēditiōsus, -a, -um	rebellious, treasonous
conscelerātus, -a, -um	criminal, wicked
cīvis, cīvis, -ium, m.	citizen
armātus, -a, -um	armed
senātus, -ūs, m.	senate
obsideō, obsidēre, obsēdī, obsessus	besiege, occupy
magistrātus, -ūs, m.	magistracy, holder of office
vīm afferre	inflict violence upon
oppugnō, oppugnāre	attack
cōtīdiē (adv.)	everyday, daily
quaerō, quaerere	(here) hold a trial or inquiry
iubeō, iubēre	command
improbō, improbāre	disapprove
crīmen, crīminis, n.	crime, criminal charge
versō, versāre	handle
iūdicium, -ī, n.	trial
requīrō, requīrere	ask
facinus, facinoris, n.	crime
audācia, -ae, f.	outrageous boldness
vocō, vocāre	call
adulescens, -ntis, m.	young man

illustris, -e	outstanding, illustrious
ingenium, -ī, n.	talent
industria, -ae, f.	diligence
grātia, -ae, f.	favor, influence
accūsō, accusāre	accuse
autem	moreover
ops, opis, f.	wealth, resources
meretrīcius, -a, -um	of a prostitute
pietās, -tātis, f.	loyalty, devotion
reprehendō, reprehendere	find fault with
muliebris, -e	pertaining to a women
libīdo, -inis, f.	lust
comprimō, comprimere	suppress, check
putō, putāre	think
labōriōsus, -a, -um	very hard-working
existimō, existimāre	judge, reckon
ōtiōsus, -a, -um	at leisure, on vacation
nē…quidem	not even
commūnis, -e	belonging to all
ōtium, -ī, n.	leisure

Exercise

1. Explain the case of *lēgem*.

   _____

   _____

2. Explain the tense and mood of *obsēderint*.

   _____

   _____

3. Explain the case of *illustrī ingeniō*.

   _____

   _____

   _____

4. Explain the tense and mood of *vocet*.

   _____

   _____

   _____

Conditional Sentences in Indirect Statement

Conditional sentences generally follow the same rules as other complex sentences. The protasis, since it is a subordinate clause, will put its verb into the subjunctive.

The apodosis, since it is an independent clause, will take a subject accusative and infinitive construction.

Poēta sī labōrat fēlix est.   If the poet works, he is happy.
Dīcit poētam sī labōret fēlīcem esse.   He says that if the poet works, he is
                                              happy.

In this simple condition, the present subjunctive **labōret** represents the original present indicative of the protasis, and the present infinitive **esse** the present indicative of the apodosis.

Dīcēbat poētam sī labōrāret fēlīcem   He said that if the poet worked, he was
   esse.   happy.

In secondary sequence it is the imperfect subjunctive **labōrāret** that represents the original present indicative.

   Future conditional sentences show an interesting simplification. Because of the limited choices of subjunctive and infinitive to represent them, the more-vivid and less-vivid varieties (see pp. 135–136) become the same:

Sī urbs *dēlēbitur*, poētae *manēbunt*.   If the city is destroyed, the poets will
                                               remain.
Dīcit sī urbs *dēlelātur*, poētās   He says that if the city is destroyed, the
   ***mansūrōs esse*.**   poets will remain.

In primary sequence the future indicative of the protasis is represented by the present subjunctive, and that of the apodosis by the future infinitive.

Sī urbs *dēleātur*, poētae *maneant*.   If the city should be destroyed, the poets
                                               would remain.
Dīcit sī urbs *dēleātur*, poētās   He says that if the city should be
   ***mansūrōs esse*.**   destroyed, the poets would remain.

The present subjunctive of the protasis remains the same, and the present subjunctive of the apodosis is represented by the future infinitive because there is really no other option.

   In secondary sequence, the protasis will take the imperfect subjunctive:

Dīcēbat sī urbs dēlērētur poētās   He said that if the city were destroyed,
   mansūrōs esse.   the poets would remain.

   Contrary-to-fact conditions obey their own rule. The subjunctive of the protasis does not change at all, regardless of sequence; it remains the same. The subjunctive of the apodosis, for both past and present contrary-to-fact sentences, is represented by the future active participle with the perfect infinitive of **sum**, that is, **fuisse**.

Present

Nisī urbs *dēlērētur*, poētae *manērent*.   If the city were not being destroyed, the
                                                 poets would remain.

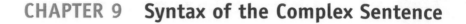

Dīcit nisī urbs *dēlērētur*, **poētās** *mansūrōs fuisse.*	He says that if the city *were not being destroyed*, the poets *would remain.*

In secondary sequence this will remain the same:

Dīcēbat nisī urbs *dēlērētur*, **poētā** *mansūrōs fuisse.*

Past

Nisī urbs *dēlēta esset*, **poētae** *mansissent.*	If the city had not been destroyed, the poets would have remained.
Dīcit nisī urbs *dēlēta esset*, **poētas** *mansūrōs fuisse.*	He says that if the city had not been destroyed, the poets would have remained.

As you can see, what distinguishes present from past contrary-to-fact conditions in indirect statement is only the tense of the subjunctive in the protasis.

Exercises

19. Translate the following sentences. Then identify what type of conditional sentence has been put into indirect statement.

   1. Dīcīt sī bellum in prōvinciā gerātur, agricolās fugere.

   _____

   _____

   _____

   2. Dīcit sī bellum in prōvinciā gerātur, agricolās fugitūrōs esse.

   _____

   _____

   _____

   3. Dīcēbat sī bellum in prōvinciā gererētur, agricolās fugitūrōs esse.

   _____

   _____

   _____

   4. Dīcit sī bellum in prōvinciā gererētur, agricolās fugitūrōs fuisse.

   _____

   _____

   _____

   5. Dīcit sī bellum in prōvinciā gestum esset, agricolās fugitūrōs fuisse.

   _____

   _____

   _____

   6. Dīcēbat sī bellum in prōvinciā gestum esset, agricolās fugitūrōs fuisse.

   _____

   _____

   _____

20. (Advanced reading) (continued from p. 160) Translate the following passage.

Etenim sī attendere dīligenter, existimāre vērē dē omnī hāc causā volueritis, sīc constituētis, iūdicēs, nec descensūrum quemquam ad hanc accūsātiōnem fuisse cui utrum vellet licēret, nec, cum descensisset, quicquam habitūrum speī fuisse nisī alicuius intolerābilī libīdine et nimis acerbō odiō nīterētur.

_____
_____
_____
_____
_____
_____
_____
_____
_____
_____

Vocabulary

etenim	and indeed
attendō, attendere	pay attention to
dīligenter (adv.)	diligently
existimō, existimāre	judge, reckon
vērē (adv.)	truly
causa, -ae, f.	case
constituō, constituere	establish, decide
iūdex, iūdicis, m.	judge
descendō, descendere, descendī, descensus	descend, stoop to
quisquam, quicquam	anyone, anything
intolerābilis, -e	unendurable, intolerable
libīdō, -inis, f.	lust
nimis (adv.)	excessively, too much
odium, -ī, n.	hatred
nītor, nītī, nīxus sum	rest on, rely upon (+ abl.)

"Fore ut" Clause

This is a subordinate clause introduced by **fore**, the future infinitive of **sum**, and the subordinating conjunction **ut**.[9] (**Fore** is actually an alternative and more commonly

_____

[9] This construction might also be considered a substantive clause of result acting as the subject of **fore**. See p. 129.

used form for **futūrum esse**, which may also be used in these constructions. See p. 67.) This construction is used in two different cases.

Because, practically speaking, there is no future passive infinitive in Latin, a future passive idea cannot be expressed in indirect statement with the normal subject accusative and infinitive construction.

Urbs a mīlitibus rēgis dēlēbitur.	The city will be destroyed by the soldiers of the king.

In such cases Latin uses the **fore ut** (less frequently, **futūrum esse ut**) with the subjunctive;

> **Dīcit** *fore ut* **urbs a mīlitibus rēgis** *dēleātur.*

Literally, this means, "He says that *it will be that* the city *is destroyed* by the soldiers of the king."

However, it is best to combine the elements in translation to convey the future passive idea:

He says that the city *will be conquered* by the soldiers of the king.

Dīcēbat *fore ut* **urbs ā mīlitibus rēgis** *dēlērētur.*	He said that the city *would be conquered* by the soldiers of the king.

Some Latin verbs lack a fourth principal part. Since the future active participle is formed from the fourth principal part, such verbs cannot form a future active infinitive and, so, will use a **fore ut** clause to express future ideas in indirect statement.

For example:

He says that the soldiers *will not be able* to destroy the city.

The verb "to be able" is **possum, posse, potuī, . . .**

Because this verbs lacks a fourth principal part, a **fore ut** construction must be used to express this idea.

Dīcit *fore ut* **mīlitēs urbem dēlēre nōn** *possint.*	He says that *it will be that* the soldiers *are unable* to destroy the city.

He says that the soldiers will be unable to destroy the city.

Dīxit fore ut mīlitēs urbem dēlēre nōn possent.	He said that the soldiers would be unable to destroy the city.

Exercise

21. Translate the following sentences.

1. Rēgīna putat fore ut poētae ā rēge interficiantur.

    _____

    _____

2. Rēgīna putābat fore ut poētae ā rēge interficerentur.

   _____

3. Rēgīna crēdit fore ut illō diē cīvēs rēgem timeant.

   _____

4. Rēgīna crēdēbat fore ut illō diē cīvēs rēgem timērent.

   _____

5. Rūmor erat fore ut rēx poētās quōs rēgīna cēlāvisset interficere nōn posset.

   _____

Impersonal Verbs

Impersonal verbs are so called because they do not have personal subjects. They take a small variety of constructions.

VERBS OF EMOTIONAL DISTRESS

Some impersonal verbs express a variety of unpleasant emotions:

piget, pigēre, piguit	to disgust
taedet, taedēre, taeduit	to weary
paenitet, paenitēre, paenituit	to cause repentance
pudet, pudēre, puduit	to shame

Such verbs put the person who feels the emotion in the accusative case.

Poētam piget.   The poet is disgusted.

The cause of the emotion may be expressed as a neuter nominative singular pronoun:

Hoc poētam piget.   This thing disgusts the poet.

The cause of the emotion may be expressed by the infinitive:

Poētam piget _vīvere_.   It disgusts the poet _to live_.

The cause of the emotion may be expressed in the genitive case:

Poētam taedet _vītae_.   _Life_ wearies the poet.
                                      The poet is weary _of life_.

Rēgem avāritiae nōn pudet.   _Avarice_ does not shame the king.
                                      The king is not ashamed _of avarice_.

Sometimes such verbs will take a subordinate clause introduced by **quod**, "that." Such clauses take the indicative:

Poētam piget *quod rēx urbem dēlēvit.*	*That the king destroyed the city* disgusts the poet.

VERBS AND EXPRESSIONS OF PERMISSION AND NECESSITY

A few impersonal verbs express necessity or obligation:

licet, licēre, licuit	to be permitted
oportet, oportēre, oportuit	to be necessary, fitting
decet, decēre, decuit	it is right
necesse est	it is necessary

Such verbs may take an accusative and infinitive construction:

Oportet poētam canere.	It is fitting that the poet sing.
Nōn licēbat mē vīvere.	It was not permitted for me to live.

They may take the infinitive with the dative case:

Necesse est poētae canere.	It is necessary for the poet to sing.

They may take a subordinate clause introduced by **ut** taking the subjunctive:

Nōn licēbat ut poētae tacērent.	It was not permitted that the poets keep silent.

VERBS OF INTEREST

There are two impersonal verbs that express "interest" or concern:

interest, interesse	it concerns, interests
rēfert, rēferre	it concerns, interests

Such verbs put the person concerned in the genitive.
The source of concern may be a neuter singular pronoun:

Hoc **rēgis rēfert.**	*This thing* concerns the king.

The source of concern may be an infinitive or accusative and infinitive:

Poētae rēfert bene *canere.*	*To sing* well concerns the poet.
Rēgis interest *poētam morī.*	*That the poet die* concerns the king.

The source of concern may be a subordinate clause introduced by **ut** taking the subjunctive:

Rēgis interest *ut poēta moriātur.*   *That the poet die* concerns the king.

The source of concern may be an indirect question:

Rēgis nōn interest *utrum opera poētae*   It does not concern the king *whether the*
sint bona.   *works of the poet are good.*

    If the person concerned would be expressed with a pronoun, i.e., "it interests *him*, *her*, etc.," rather than use that pronoun in the genitive, these verbs use the possessive adjective in the feminine ablative singular:[10]

Meā *rēfert* ut poētae serventur.   *It concerns me* that the poets be saved.
Vestrā *interest* utrum rēx sit dēmēns.   *It concerns you* whether the king is
                                                    insane.

Exercises

22.   Translate the following.

    1. Quod rēx bellum parat cīvēs taedet.

    ———————————————————————————

    2. Poētae nōn rēfert utrum rēx librōs dēleat.

    ———————————————————————————

    3. Poēta dīxit fore ut omnēs librōs dēlērentur.

    ———————————————————————————

    4. Avāritiae rēgis omnēs piget.

    ———————————————————————————

    5. Omnium interest ut lībertās servētur.

    ———————————————————————————

    6. Taedet rēgīnam rēgem vidēre.

    ———————————————————————————

    7. Tuā maximē interest abīre.

    ———————————————————————————

---

[10] This feminine ablative singular is understood to agree with the prefix **rē-**, the ablative singular of the noun **rēs**. Originally the expression was **mea rēs fert**—"my interest bears"—the **rēs** combining with **fert** to produce **rēfert**, in which the **rē** perhaps appeared to have become ablative and occasioned the change from **mea** to **meā**. However, this use of the feminine ablative singular of the possessive also works for the verb **interest**, with no **rē** anywhere in sight.

8. Necesse erit omnibus cīvibus hunc librum legere.

_____

_____

9. Necesse erit ut hic liber ab omnibus cīvibus legātur.

_____

_____

10. Nōn licēbat nōbīs ut in pāce vīverēmus.

_____

_____

23. Translate the following sentences.

1. In tantā laetitiā cunctae cīvitātis mē ūnum tristem esse oportēbat?

_____

_____

2. Nōn tamen pigēbit vel inc|onditā ac rude vōce memoriam priōris servitūtis ac testimōnium praesentium bonōrum composuisse.

_____

_____

_____

_____

3. Neque mē mīlitum neque vōs ducis paenituit.

_____

_____

4. Quandō dēnique fuit ut quod licet nōn licēret?

_____

_____

5. Ad mortem tē, Catilīna, dūcī iussū cōnsulis iam prīdem oportēbat; in tē cōnferrī pestem quam tū in nōs māchināris.

_____

_____

_____

_____

6. Quid rēfert utrum voluerim fierī an gaudeām factum?

_____

_____

Vocabulary

tantus, -a, -um	so great
laetitia, -ae, f.	happiness
cunctus, -a, -um	all, the whole
cīvitās, -tātis, f.	citizenry, state
tristis, -e	depressed, sad
vel	even

inconditus, -a, -um	unpolished, rough
rudis, -e	crude, unfinished
vōx, vōcis, f.	voice
memoria, -ae, f.	memory, record
prior, prius	earlier, prior
servitūs, -tūtis, f.	slavery
testimōnium, ī, n.	testimony
praesēns, -ntis	present, at hand
compōnō, compōnere, composuī, compositus	compose, write
dux, ducis, m.	leader
dēnique	finally
mors, mortis, -ium, f.	death
Catilīna, -ae, m.	Catiline
dūcō, dūcere	lead
iussū (abl.)	by order of (+ gen.)
cōnsul, cōnsulis, m.	consul
iam prīdem	for a long time already
conferō, conferre	bring, bestow, confer
pestis, pestis, f.	pestilence, destruction
māchinor, māchinārī, māchinātus sum	devise, contrive
gaudeō, gaudēre, gāvīsus sum	be happy

The Infinitive

The infinitive is a verbal noun, and as such it may be the subject of a sentence:

Placet *dormīre.*	It is pleasing *to sleep.*
Vīdisse **lībertātem bonum est.**	It is good *to have seen* liberty.

Note that the adjective **bonum** takes the neuter singular. As nouns, infinitives are treated as neuter singular.

The infinitive may be the object of a transitive[11] verb:

Poēta *canere* **optat.**	The poet chooses *to sing.*
Morī **praeferimus.**	We prefer *to die.*

Some intransitive[12] verbs, such as **possum**, take the infinitive:

Hominēs ērectī *ambulāre* **possunt.**	Men are able *to walk* upright.

---

[11] A transitive verb is one that takes a direct object.
[12] An intransitive verb is one that cannot take a direct object.

Such an infinitive is felt to complete the meaning of the verb and is called a *complementary infinitive*.

The infinitive may take a nominative subject and act as the main verb of a sentence:

Mīlitēs clāmāre, fugere, capī.   The soldiers shouted, fled, were
                                             captured.

Because such usages of the infinitive occur most often among writers of historical narrative, they are called *historical infinitives*. Usually they appear in groups.

Gerund and Gerundive

The gerund serves as the verbal noun in the genitive, dative, and ablative cases, and in the accusative with certain prepositions. It will have the normal syntax associated with these different cases.

Poētae est amor *canendī.*   The poet has a love *of singing*.

Here the gerund **canendī** is an objective genitive.

Interficiendō **rēx cīvēs terret.**   The king terrifies the inhabitants *by
                                                killing*.

Here the gerund **interficiendō** is an ablative of means.

Although it is a verbal noun, the gerund tends not to govern a direct object. To express a direct object relationship, Latin uses the gerundive. The gerundive is a verbal adjective that, instead of governing a direct object in the accusative case, agrees with its noun in gender, number, and case:

Interficiendīs poētīs **rēx cīvēs terret.**   The king will terrify the citizens *by
                                                   killing poets*.

The phrase **interficiendīs poētīs** is in the ablative case as an ablative of means. It expresses the means by which the king will terrify the citizens. Though "the poets" would normally be expressed as a direct object in any other type of verbal expression, with the gerundive such a relationship is usually expressed by noun-adjective agreement.

Mīlitibus est timor *urbis dēlendae.*   The soldiers have a fear *of destroying the
                                               city.*

Again, in any other verbal expression, "the city" would be the direct object of the verb "to destroy":

Mīlitēs timent *urbem* **dēlēre.**   The soldiers are afraid to destroy the
                                                city.

In the first example, however, the phrase **urbis dēlendae** functions as an objective genitive, so the noun and gerundive agree in that case.

The gerund and the gerundive in the accusative case with the preposition **ad** express purpose:

Rēx mīlitēs mittit *ad urbem delendam.*   The king sends soldiers *for the purpose of destroying the city.*

This meaning can also be expressed with the genitive followed by the preposition **causā:**[13]

Rēx mīlitēs mittit *urbis dēlendae causā.*   The king sends soldiers *for the sake of destroying the city.*

Supine

The supine is a verbal noun that exists only in the accusative and ablative cases (see Chapter 4, verbal noun section). The accusative is used to express purpose with a verb of motion:

Rēx mīlitēs mittit urbem *dēlētum.*   The king sends soldiers *to destroy* the city.

The ablative is used to express respect or specification:

mīrābile dictū   (a thing) wonderful *to say.*

Exercises

24. Translate the following.

1. Dulce est vīvere?

   _____

2. Ad prōvinciam ībō bellum vīsum.

   _____

3. Ad prōvinciam ībō ad bellum videndum.

   _____

4. Ad prōvinciam ībō bellī videndī causā.

   _____

5. Poētās interficere erat terribile factū.

   _____

---

[13] This is really the ablative of the noun **causa**, which has this independent usage. It follows a noun in the genitive case and means "for the sake of."

6. In urbe manēre poēta volēbat.

_____

_____

7. Mīlitēs urbem dēlēre timent.

_____

_____

8. Lībertātis omnium dēlendae causā rēx poētās interficere voluit.

_____

_____

25. Translate the following sentences.

1. O rem nōn modō vīsū foedam sed etiam audītū!

_____

_____

2. Nōn igitur mīliēns perīre est melius quam in suā cīvitāte sine armātōrum praesidiō nōn posse vīvere?

_____

_____

_____

3. Diēs iam mē dēficiat sī quae dīcī in eam sententiam possunt cōner exprōmere.

_____

_____

_____

4. Pro meā perpetuā cupiditāte vetrae dīgnitātis retinendae et augendae quaesō ōrōque vōs, patrēs, conscriptī, ut prīmō, etsī erit vel acerbum audītū vel incrēdibile ā Cicerōne dictum, accipiātis sine offensiōne quod dīxerō, nēve id prius quam quāle sit explicāverō repudiētis.

_____

_____

_____

_____

_____

_____

Vocabulary

nōn modo	not only
foedus, -a, -um	foul
sed etiam	but also
igitur (adv.)	therefore
mīliēns (adv.)	a thousand times
pereō, perīre	die, perish
cīvitās, -tātis, f.	citizenry, state

armātus, -a, -um	armed
vīvo, vīvere	live
praesidium, -ī, n.	protection
dēficiō, dēficere	be lacking, run out
sententia, -ae, f.	thought, opinion
cōnor, cōnārī, cōnātus sum	try, attempt (+ inf.)
exprōmō, exprōmere	bring out, reveal
perpetuus, -a, -um	perpetual
cupiditās, -tātis, f.	desire
dīgnitās, -tātis, f.	dignity, prestige
retineō, retinēre	retain, keep, maintain
augeō, augēre	increase
quaesō	I ask
patrēs cōnscriptī	senators
prīmō (adv.)	first
vel ... vel	either ... or
acerbus, -a, -um	bitter
incrēdibilis, -e	incredible
Cicerō, -ōnis, m.	Cicero
accipiō, accipere	accept, hear
offensiō, -ōnis, f.	offense
nēve	and not (+ subj.)
quālis, -e	how, of what kind
explicō, explicāre	explain
repudiō, repudiāre	reject, repudiate

Answers to Exercises

Chapter 1

1. 1. Vocative
   2. Nominative
   3. Genitive
   4. Accusative
   5. Dative
   6. Ablative

2.

	Sing.	*Pl.*
Nom.	aqua	aquae
Gen.	aquae	aquārum
Dat.	aquae	aquīs
Acc.	aquam	aquās
Abl.	aquā	aquīs

3. 1. puellās
   2. mēnsārum, mēnsīs
   3. poētae
   4. terrīs
   5. aquārum, aquīs
   6. fēminārum, fēminīs
   7. terrās
   8. pecūniae

4. 1. puella
   2. terram
   3. poētae, poētā
   4. aquae
   5. mēnsae, mēnsā
   6. terra
   7. īnsulae
   8. lūna

5. 1.

	Sing.	*Pl.*
Nom.	saxum	saxa
Gen.	saxī	saxōrum
Dat.	saxō	saxīs
Acc.	saxum	saxa
Abl.	saxō	saxīs

   2.

	Sing.	*Pl.*
Nom.	puer	puerī
Gen.	puerī	puerōrum
Dat.	puerō	puerīs
Acc.	puerum	puerōs
Abl.	puerō	puerīs
Voc.	puer	puerī

   3.

	Sing.	*Pl.*
Nom.	amīcus	amīcī
Gen.	amīcī	amīcōrum
Dat.	amīcō	amīcīs
Acc.	amīcum	amīcōs
Abl.	amīcō	amīcīs
Voc.	amīce	amīcī

6. 1. regna, regna
   2. gladiōrum
   3. virīs, virīs
   4. librī
   5. numerōs
   6. gaudia, gaudia
   7. puerī
   8. regna

7. 1. virī
   2. gladium
   3. bellum, bellum
   4. ventus
   5. amīcō, amīcō
   6. vir
   7. numerum
   8. regnī

8.

1.	*Sing.*	*Pl.*
Nom.	corpus	corpora
Gen.	corporis	corporum
Dat.	corporī	corporibus
Acc.	corpus	corpora
Abl.	corpore	corporibus

2.	*Sing.*	*Pl.*
Nom.	mēns	mentēs
Gen.	mentis	mentium
Dat.	mentī	mentibus
Acc.	mentem	mentēs/mentīs
Abl.	mente	mentibus

3.	*Sing.*	*Pl.*
Nom.	dolor	dolōrēs
Gen.	dolōris	dolōrum

Dat.   dolōrī   dolōribus
Acc.   dolōrem   dolōrēs
Abl.   dolōre   dolōribus

9. 1. urbēs, urbīs (i-stem)
2. rēgibus
3. vōcum
4. animālibus, animālibus
5. flūmina, flūmina
6. urbium
7. noctēs
8. amōribus

10. 1. sīdus, sīdus
2. voluptātī, voluptāte
3. urbs, urbem
4. dolōris
5. montem
6. mentis
7. animal, animal
8. nāvis
9. amōrī, amōre

11.
	Sing.	*Pl.*
1. Nom.	speciēs	speciēs
Gen.	speciēī	speciērum
Dat.	speciēī	speciēbus
Acc.	speciem	speciēs
Abl.	speciē	speciēbus
2. Nom.	manus	manūs
Gen.	manūs	manuum
Dat.	manuī	manibus
Acc.	manum	manūs
Abl.	manū	manibus

12. 1. rēs, rēs
2. diērum
3. frūctuum
4. frūctibus
5. genus 2x, genibus 2x

13. 1. genū
2. ūsūs
3. reī
4. diēī, diē
5. rēs, rem

14. 1. first
2. fifth
3. third

4. third
5. fourth
6. second
7. second
8. first
9. third
10. third

15. 1. liberty (direct object)
2. of the horsemen
3. from, with, in, by rocks/to, for rocks
4. of the poet, for the poet, the poets (subject)
5. fields (direct object)
6. example (subject or direct object)
7. of the shore
8. of the appearance/to, for appearance
9. to, for the queens/from, with, in, by queens
10. the appearance of liberty
11. the king of the poets
12. rocks of the field

16. 1. currūs
2. exemplāribus
3. rēgīnārum, rēgīnīs
4. equitibus
5. lītora

17. 1. poētae, poētā
2. agrī
3. saxum, saxum
4. lībertātis
5. rēgīnam

18.
1.	puella	puellae	
	puellae	puellārum	
	puellae	puellīs	
	puellam	puellās	
	puellā	puellīs	
2.	dolor	dolōrēs	
	dolōris	dolōrum	
	dolōrī	dolōribus	
	dolōrem	dolōrēs	
	dolōre	dolōribus	
3.	bellum	bella	
	bellī	bellōrum	
	bellō	bellīs	
	bellum	bella	
	bellō	bellīs	

4. spīritus   spīritūs
   spīritūs   spīrituum
   spīrituī   spīritibus
   spīritum   spīritūs
   spīritū   spīritibus

5. rēs   rēs
   reī   rērum
   reī   rēbus
   rem   rēs
   rē   rēbus

6. urbs   urbēs
   urbis   urbium
   urbī   urbibus
   urbem   urbēs, urbīs
   urbe   urbibus

Chapter 2

1.
1. magnus
2. magnae
3. magnīs, magnīs
4. magnōrum
5. magnō
6. magnī, magnī, magnōs
7. magna, magnae, magnās
8. magnōrum
9. magna
10. magnārum

2.
1. rēx bonus   rēgēs bonī
   rēgis bonī   rēgum bonōrum
   rēgī bonō   rēgibus bonīs
   rēgem bonum   rēgēs bonōs
   rēge bonō   rēgibus bonīs
       voc. sing.   rēx bone

2. urbs pulchra   urbēs pulchrae
   urbis pulchrae   urbium pulchrārum
   urbī pulchrae   urbibus pulchrīs
   urbem pulchram   urbēs/urbīs pulchrās
   urbe pulchrā   urbibus pulchrīs

3. bellum dūrum   bella dūra
   bellī dūrī   bellōrum dūrōrum
   bellō dūrō   bellīs dūrīs
   bellum dūrum   bella dūra
   bellō dūrō   bellīs dūrīs

3.
1. nōbilī
2. nōbilibus
3. nōbile 2x
4. nōbilium
5. nōbilēs, nōbilēs, nōbilīs
6. nōbilia 2x
7. nōbilis
8. nōbilis, nōbilī
9. nōbilem
10. nōbilēs, nōbilīs

4.
1. puella dēmēns   puellae dēmentēs
   puellae dēmentis   puellārum dēmentium
   puellae dēmentī   puellīs dēmentibus
   puellam dēmentem   puellās dēmentēs, dēmentīs
   puellā dēmentī   puellīs dēmentibus

2. rēs facilis   rēs facilēs
   reī facilis   rērum facilium
   reī facilī   rēbus facilibus
   rem facilem   rēs facilēs, facilīs
   rē facilī   rēbus facilibus

5.
1. malae, grandis or malae, grandī or malae, grandēs
2. malī, grandis or malī, grandēs
3. mala, grandia 2x
4. malīs, grandibus 2x
5. malārum, grandium
6. malī, grandēs or malōs, grandēs/grandīs
7. malus, grandis
8. malae, grandis or malae, grandēs or malae, grandēs/grandīs
9. malum, grande 2x
10. malārum, grandium
11. malae, grandis
12. malō, grandī
13. malōrum, grandium
14. malōs, grandēs/grandīs
15. malum, grande 2x

6.
1. tōtīus, tōtī
2. tōtā
3. tōtus
4. tōtīus
5. tōtīus, tōtī
6. tōtīus, tōtī
7. tōtō

7.
1. poēta grandior   poētae grandiōrēs
   poētae grandiōris   poētārum grandiōrum
   poētae grandiōrī   poētis grandiōribus
   poētam grandiōrem   poētās grandiōrēs/-īs
   poētā grandiōrī(-e)   poētīs grandiōribus

8. 1. rēs facillima   rēs facillimae
   rēī facillimae   rērum facillimārum
   rēī facillimae   rēbus facillimīs
   rem facillimam   rēs facillimās
   rē facillimā   rēbus facillimīs

   2. rēgīna miserrima   rēgīnae miserrimae
   rēgīnae miserrimae   rēgīnārum miserrimārum
   reginae miserrimae   rēgīnīs miserrimīs
   rēgīnam miserrimam   rēgīnās miserrimās
   rēgīnā miserrimā   rēgīnae miserrimīs

9. 1. sharp breath
   2. most humble voices
   3. a most hard king
   4. the greatest luxury
   5. the least faith
   6. a better mind
   7. the best wind
   8. the greater son
   9. a more insane joy
   10. most noble liberty
   11. of the most beautiful ships
   12. of the worst animal

Chapter 3

1. 1. ego
   2. nōs
   3. vōs
   4. tū

2. 1. nōs
   2. sē
   3. vōs
   4. sē

3. 1. haec
   2. illum
   3. eārum
   4. ipsa, ipsae, ipsās
   5. eōrundem
   6. hīs
   7. huius
   8. illīs, illīs
   9. eāsdem
   10. ipsa

4. 1. that queen
   2. you (pl.) yourselves
   3. the same wind
   4. these girls
   5. those rocks
   6. that man lives
   7. she herself comes
   8. that woman herself comes
   9. I saw the brother of this man
   10. That man will live, this one will die.

5. 1. cui
   2. cuius
   3. quī, quōs
   4. cuius, quī
   5. cuius, quī
   6. quārum
   7. quibus 2x
   8. quōs
   9. quōrum
   10. quibus 2x

6. 1. aliquī
   2. quōsque
   3. quaedam
   4. alicuius
   5. quaeque

7. 1. some money
   2. each queen
   3. a certain war

Chapter 4

1. 1. dūcō
   dūcis
   dūcit
   dūcimus
   dūcitis
   dūcunt
   2. veniō
   venīs
   venit
   venīmus
   venītis
   veniunt
   3. iaciō
   iacis
   iacit
   iacimus
   iacitis
   iaciunt

Answers to Exercises

2. 1. impleor
implēris/implēre
implētur
implēmur
implēminī
implentur
2. pellor
pelleris/pellere
pellitur
pellimur
pelliminī
pelluntur
3. paror
parāris/parāre
parātur
parāmur
parāminī
parantur

3. 1. 1st person plural active: we fill
2. 3rd person singular passive:
he, she, it is led
3. 3rd person plural active: they hurl
4. 3rd person plural passive:
they are being prepared
5. 2nd person singular active: you push
6. 2nd person singular passive:
you are being pushed
7. 2nd person plural passive:
you (pl.) are being hurled
8. 2nd person plural active: you (pl.) prepare
9. 3rd person plural active: they lead
10. 1st person plural passive: we are filled

4. 1. implēbam
implēbās
implēbat
implēbāmus
implēbātis
implēbant
2. pellēbam
pellēbās
pellēbat
pellēbāmus
pellēbātis
pellēbant
3. veniēbam
veniēbās
veniēbat
veniēbāmus
veniēbātis
veniēbant

5. 1. dūcēbar
dūcēbāris/dūcēbāre
dūcēbātur
dūcēbāmur
dūcēbāminī
dūcēbantur
2. habēbar
habēbāris/habēbāre
habēbātur
habēbāmur
habēbāminī
habebantur

6. 1. 1st person plural passive:
we were being pushed
2. 1st person plural active: we were holding
3. 1st person singular active: I was leading
4. 2nd person plural passive:
you (pl.) were being pushed
5. 3rd person plural passive:
they were being filled
6. 3rd person plural active: they were coming
7. 3rd person singular passive:
he, she, it was being held
8. 3rd person singular active:
he, she, it was filling

7. 1. parābō
parābis
parābit
parābimus
parābitis
parābunt
2. dūcam
dūcēs
dūcet
dūcēmus
dūcētis
dūcent

8. 1. implēbor
implēberis/implēbere
implēbitur
implēbimur
implēbiminī
implēbuntur

2. audiar
   audiēris/audiēre
   audiētur
   audiēmur
   audiēminī
   audientur

9. 1. 2nd person singular active:
      you will prepare
   2. 1st person singular active: I will fill
   3. 1st person plural passive: we will be led
   4. 3rd person singular passive:
      he, she, it will be heard
   5. 1st person singular active: I will push
   6. 3rd person plural passive:
      they will be prepared
   7. 2nd person plural active:
      you (pl.) will have
   8. 1st person plural active: we will push
   9. 2nd person singular passive:
      you will be filled
   10. 2nd person plural passive:
       you (pl.) will be led

10. 1. parem
       parēs
       paret
       parēmus
       parētis
       parent
    2. faciam
       faciās
       faciat
       faciāmus
       faciātis
       faciant

11. 1. habear
       habeāris/habeāre
       habeātur
       habeāmur
       habeāminī
       habeantur
    2. dūcar
       dūcāris/dūcāre
       dūcātur
       dūcāmur
       dūcāminī
       dūcantur

12. facerem
    facerēs
    faceret
    facerēmus
    facerētis
    facerent

13. dūcerer
    dūcerēris/dūcerēre
    dūcerētur
    dūcerēmur
    dūcerēminī
    dūcerentur

14. 1. 1st person plural present indicative active
    2. 2nd person plural present subjunctive
       active
    3. 3rd person singular imperfect indicative
       active
    4. 3rd person singular present subjunctive
       passive
    5. 3rd person plural future indicative active
    6. 2nd person singular imperfect subjunctive
       active
    7. 2nd person singular future indicative active
    8. 2nd person plural present subjunctive
       active
    9. 2nd person plural present indicative active
    10. 1st person singular present subjunctive or
        future indicative active
    11. 2nd person singular future indicative
        passive
    12. 2nd person singular imperfect subjunctive
        active
    13. 2nd person singular future indicative
        passive
    14. 2nd person singular present indicative
        passive or present active infinitive
        or present imperative passive,
        singular
    15. 2nd person singular present subjunctive
        passive
    16. present imperative active plural
    17. present imperative active, singular
    18. 1st person singular future indicative
        passive
    19. 1st person plural future indicative passive
    20. 1st person plural imperfect indicative
        passive
    21. 1st person singular future indicative active

22. 1st person plural present subjunctive active
23. 2nd person plural present indicative active
24. 2nd person plural present subjunctive passive
25. 2nd person singular imperfect indicative active
26. 2nd person plural future indicative active
27. present imperative active, plural
28. future imperative active, singular
29. 1st person plural present indicative active
30. 1st person plural imperfect indicative passive
31. 2nd person singular present indicative passive or present infinitive active or present imperative passive, singular
32. 2nd person singular imperfect subjunctive passive
33. present imperative active, singular

15.
1. he, she, it says
2. you will hurl
3. they push
4. I will make
5. they were being destroyed
6. we say
7. manage!
8. you will be pushed
9. you are led/be led!/to lead
10. you (pl.) were coming
11. he, she, it walks
12. he, she it will be filled
13. they will make
14. you (pl.) were being filled
15. you (pl.) are being captured/be captured!
16. hear!
17. let him command/or command
18. you have
19. it will be waged
20. we walk

16.
1. dīcitur
2. dūcāmur
3. gerēminī
4. dūciminī
5. pellēbar
6. iubērētur
7. dēlēberis/dēlēbere
8. capere
9. iacimur
10. audiar

17.
1. iubeō
2. gerēbāmus
3. capitis
4. pellet
5. dēlērēs
6. implēbis
7. capis/cape
8. dīcunt
9. habēbātis
10. iacerēmus

18.
1. dēlet
2. caperis/capere
3. faciāmus
4. gerētis
5. veniēbātis
6. dicāmus/dīcēmus
7. pellerem
8. implēbunt
9. dūcēs
10. habēbiminī

19.
1. 1st person singular future perfect indicative active
2. 1st person plural pluperfect subjunctive active
3. 3rd person singular future perfect indicative or perfect subjunctive active
4. 1st person singular perfect subjunctive active
5. 2nd person singular perfect indicative active
6. 3rd person plural perfect indicative active
7. 3rd person plural pluperfect indicative active
8. 3rd person plural future perfect indicative or perfect subjunctive active
9. 2nd person plural perfect indicative active
10. 3rd person singular pluperfect subjunctive active

20.
1. you (pl.) had filled
2. I will have made
3. you came/you have come
4. I loved/I have loved
5. you (pl.) will have hurled
6. you (pl.) had hurled
7. you (pl.) hurled/you (pl.) have hurled
8. they pushed/they have pushed
9. I said/I have said
10. we said/we have said

21.
1. 3rd person singular perfect indicative passive
2. 3rd person singular pluperfect indicative passive
3. 3rd person plural perfect indicative passive
4. 1st person singular perfect indicative passive
5. 1st person plural perfect indicative passive
6. 2nd person singular pluperfect subjective passive
7. 3rd person plural future perfect indicative passive
8. 3rd person plural perfect subjective passive
9. 3rd person singular pluperfect subjective passive
10. 3rd person plural pluperfect indicative passive

22.
1. it was filled/it has been filled
2. she had been filled
3. we were commanded/we have been commanded
4. they will have been destroyed
5. they had been pushed
6. it will have been hurled
7. they had been captured
8. she has been captured
9. they will have been loved
10. I had been loved

23.
1. captus, -a, -um eris/captus, -a, -um sīs
2. captus, -a, -um sim
3. dēlētī, -ae, -a estis
4. iactī, -ae, -ī erāmus
5. pulsus, -a, -um esset
6. implētus, -a, -um est
7. implētus, -a, -um erit/implētus, -a, -um sit
8. implētus, -a, -um erat
9. implētī, -ae, -a essēmus
10. ductī, -ae, -a sunt

24.
1. dūxissētis
2. cēperat
3. cēpimus
4. cēperō
5. dūxerit
6. dēlēverit
7. dēlēvērunt
8. dēlēverant
9. dēlēverint
10. dēlēvisset

25.
1. 3rd person plural perfect indicative active
   they loved/they have loved
2. 3rd person plural future perfect indicative passive
   they will have been led
3. 3rd person plural future perfect indicative active[1]
   he will have walked
4. 2nd person singular perfect indicative active
   you commanded/you have commanded
5. 3rd person singular perfect indicative passive
   he was ordered/he has been ordered
6. 3rd person singular pluperfect indicative passive
   it had been destroyed
7. 1st person plural pluperfect indicative active
   we had destroyed
8. 2nd person plural perfect indicative active
   you (person plural) filled/you (person plural) have filled
9. 2nd person plural pluperfect indicative active
   you (person plural) had pushed
10. 2nd person plural future perfect indicative active
    you (person plural) will have captured
11. 2nd person singular imp. indicative active
    you were walking
12. 1st person singular future indicative active[2]
    I will push
13. 2nd person plural future indicative active
    you (person plural) will fill
14. 3rd person plural future indicative active
    they will push
15. 2nd person singular future indicative passive
    you will be pushed

---

[1] This form could also be the perfect subjunctive, but this should not be translated in isolation.
[2] This form could also be present subjunctive. See above.

Answers to Exercises

16. 2nd person singular future indicative passive
you will be pushed
17. 2nd person plural present indicative passive
you (person plural) are led
18. 2nd person plural imperative indicative passive
you (person plural) were being led
19. 3rd person plural future indicative passive
they will be led
20. 1st person plural present indicative passive
we are filled
21. 3rd person singular imperative indicative passive
he, she, it was being filled
22. 3rd person plural future indicative active
they will fill
23. 3rd person plural future indicative passive
they will be filled
24. 1st person singular future indicative active
I will destroy
25. 2nd person singular imperative indicative passive
you were being captured
26. present imperative active person singular
capture!
27. 2nd person singular present indicative passive
you are captured
present imperative person singular, passive
be captured!
present infinitive active
to capture
28. 3rd person singular present indicative active
he, she, it hurls
29. 3rd person plural future indicative active
they will hurl
30. 3rd person singular future indicative passive
he, she, it will be hurled
31. 3rd person plural perfect indicative passive
they were hurled/they have been hurled
32. 2nd prson plural future perfect indicative active[3]
you (person plural) will have hurled
33. 3rd person singular imperfect indicative passive
he, she, it was being hurled

34. 3rd person singular pluperfect indicative passive
they had been hurled

26. 1. 1st person singular perfect active
2. 2nd person plural present passive
3. 2nd person plural pluperfect active
4. 2nd person plural pluperfect passive
5. 2nd person singular imperative passive
6. 3rd person singular perfect passive
7. 3rd person plural imperfect active
8. 1st person plural present passive
9. 2nd person plural perfect active
10. 3rd person singular pluperfect active
11. 3rd person singular imperative passive
12. 2nd person singular present passive
13. 3rd person plural perfect passive
14. 3rd person plural imperative passive
15. 3rd person singular present active
16. 2nd person plural present active
17. 1st person plural imperative passive
18. 2nd person singular pluperfect active
19. 1st person singular pluperfect passive
20. 1st person singular perfect active

27. 1. perfect active infinitive
to have had
2. present passive infinitive
to be waged
3. perfect passive infinitive
to have been driven
4. present active infinitive
to hurl
5. present passive infinitive
to be destroyed
6. future active infinitive
to be about to destroy
7. perfect active infinitive
to have destroyed

28. 1. capturing
2. the soldier capturing
3. the soldier capturing the city
4. the soldier about to capture the city
5. captured
6. the captured city
7. the city captured by the soldier
8. the city captured by the capturing soldier
9. the city captured by the soldier about to say something

---

[3] The form is also perfect subjunctive. Do not translate.

29. 1. the city has to be destroyed
2. the cities had to be destroyed
3. the cities will have to be destroyed
4. the men are about to destroy the city
5. the men were about to destroy the city
6. the men will be about to destroy the city

30. 1. they had slipped
2. we will speak
3. you use
4. you will use
5. I am about to die
6. you (person plural) were fearing
7. you (person plural) will fear
8. you (person plural) will have slipped
9. you will try
10. it has to be gained
11. they speak
12. he, she, it uses

31. 1. 3rd person singular present subjective
2. 2nd person plural imperative subjective
3. 3rd person plural perfect subjective
4. 1st person plural present subjective
5. 2nd person singular present subjective
6. 1st person singular pluperfect subjective
7. 1st person plural present subjective
8. 1st person plural future indicative
9. 1st person plural present indicative
10. 2nd person plural present indicative active

32. 1. we will be
2. they do not wish
3. you (person plural) will be able
4. they are able
5. you (person plural) wish
6. he, she, it will go
7. you carry
8. we are made
9. you are carried
10. you (person plural) prefer
11. we do not wish
12. I was going
13. you were able
14. you (person plural) are
15. to be unwilling
16. to be made
17. you (person plural) are carried
18. you go
19. I will wish
20. they prefer
21. he, she, it was unwilling

22. to carry
23. going
24. you (person plural) are able
25. to be able

Chapter 5

1. 1. nōbiliter   nōbilius   nōbilissimē
2. acerbē   acerbius   acerbissimē
3. miserē   miserius   miserrimē
4. male   peius   pessimē
5. bene   melius   optimē

2. 1. under the moon
2. after the war
3. by the king
4. around the city
5. through the fields
6. without love
7. out of the water
8. with avarice
9. down from the mountains
10. against the soldiers
11. on account of money
12. on behalf of the queen
13. across the river
14. before the day
15. by the poet

Chapter 6

1. 1. The boy is the son of the sailor.
predicate nominative
2. Avarice is the love of money.
objective genitive
3. The joy of the friends is great.
predicate nominative
4. I hear the great joy of the friends.
subjective genitive
5. the sword of the daughter
possessive genitive
6. the breath of God
subjective genitive
7. the pain of the blind slaves
subjective genitive
8. It is characteristic of sons to love their
fathers.
predicate genitive
9. an animal of large horns
genitive of description

Answers to Exercises

10. horns of animals
    possessive genitive
11. I reckon that queen (the value) of nothing.
    genitive of indefinite value

2. 1. Therefore as in seeds is the cause of trees and plants, so you were the cause of this most distressing war.
2. As Helen for the Trojans, so that man was the cause of war for this republic, the cause of pestilence and destruction.
3. Both the name of peace is sweet and the thing itself beneficial; but between peace and slavery there is a great difference. Peace is tranquil liberty, slavery the most extreme of all evil things, to be repelled not only by war but even death.
4. There was a very great amount of wine, a great quantity of the best silver.... Of these things within a few days there was nothing.
5. It is characteristic of a commander to conquer with planning no less than with the sword.
6. The recollection of slavery will make liberty more pleaperson singular
7. He does not think your gifts of such great (value).

3. 1. They prepare those things which are of use to the town.
2. That man was in charge of the Roman citadel.
3. What reason did you bring to the Roman people?
4. To some planning was lacking, to others spirit, to others opportunity; to no one the will (was lacking).
5. Let us prefer death to slavery.

4. 1. I do not have a sword.
    dat. of the possessor
2. The king was giving money to the soldiers.
    dat. indirect object
3. The ship had to be destroyed by the poets.
    dat. of agent
4. The city of great luxury had to be destroyed by the sailors.
    dat. of agent
5. That water is harmful to children.
    dat. with intransitive verb

6. Waves are a source of great danger to sailors.
    predicate dative
7. He put the army behind the mountains.
    dat. with compound verb

5. 1. Money will destroy friendship.
    direct object
2. I walked all night.
    acc. of extent of time
3. We do not wish to go a difficult road.
    internal accusative
4. The women advanced to Rome.
    acc. of place to which
5. I say that money destroys friendship.
    acc. subject of an infinitive
6. He says that the men are shouting.
    acc. subject of an infinitive
7. Avarice destroyed the mind of the king.
    direct object
8. For many years avarice was destroying the mind of the king.
    acc. of extent of time.

6. 1. Indeed the republic certainly has most noble young men prepared as defenders.
2. But who can tolerate this most foul beast or how? What is there in Antonius beyond lust, cruelty, arrogance, audacity?
3. Put before your eyes the happiness of the senate and the Roman people.
4. Already I had seen that an evil war against the altars and hearths, against our life and fortunes was not being prepared, but waged by a profligate and desperate man.
5. But for how many days in that villa did you most foully revel!
6. O the criminal baseness of the man, o the shamelessness, the worthlessness, the lust not to be borne!

7. 1. The animal is bigger than the boy.
    abl. of comparison
2. The animals are led by the boy.
    abl. of personal agent
3. The women came to the sea with great care.
    abl. of manner
4. The women came from Rome.
    abl. of place from which

5. You drove out the poet because of avarice.
   abl. of cause
6. You drove out the poet with a sword.
   abl. of means
7. With the poets singing, the gods heard us.
   abl. absolute
8. That year there were many wars in the land.
   abl. of time when
9. The king is much more insane than the queen.
   abl. of degree of difference
10. I fear animals with large horns.
    abl. of description
11. The queen ran out of the city because of fear.
    abl. of cause

8. 1. They are indeed of excellent mind, the best advice, outstanding agreement.
2. All these men differ among themselves in respect to language, customs, laws.
3. But Antonius is being held, pressed, pressured now by those troops which we already have, soon by those which within a few days the new consuls will prepare.
4. For who is more chaste than this young man, who more modest, what more illustrious example do we have in our youth of the ancient sanctity?
5. Already that man had brought the habit of being a slave to a free state, partly because of fear, partly because of suffering. I can compare you with that man in respect to lust of dominating, but in respect to other things in no way must you be compared with him.
6. With these men being the producers and leaders, with the gods helping, with us keeping watch and providing many things for the future, with the Roman people being in agreement, we will indeed be free within a short time. Moreover the recollection of slavery will make liberty more pleaperson singular

Chapter 7

1. 1. Evil men love money.
2. Much money is better than love.
3. Much money is much better than much love.

4. Gold is the most beautiful of all good things.
5. I say that water is as beautiful as possible.
6. The wretched poet was shouting about the avarice of the Romans.
7. The poet was shouting wretchedly about the avarice of the Romans.

2. 1. All of your plans are clearer to us than light.
2. But who is able to bear this most foul beast?
3. Indeed the republic certainly has most noble young men prepared as defenders.
4. Who at any time (was) more pleasing to rather famous men, who more conjoined with rather foul men? What citizen ever of better parts, what enemy more horrible to this state? Who more dirty in his pleasures, who more patient in labors? Who more greedy in rapacity, who more unrestrained in bribery?

Chapter 8

1. 1. The sailor sees.
2. The sailor will see the mountain.
3. The sailor saw the mountain with his eyes.
4. The sailor had seen the war in the mountains with his eyes.
5. With many tears the wretched sailor was seeing the extremely bad war in the mountains of the kingdom.
6. The mountain is seen.
7. The mountain is seen by the sailor.
8. The war is seen by the sailor in the mountains.

2. 1. The king terrifies the citizens.
2. The king will terrify the citizens.
3. The king terrified the citizens.
4. The king will have terrified the citizens.
5. The king had terrified the citizens.
6. The king was terrifying the citizens.

3. 1. We will proceed with arguments, we will refute the charges with proofs clearer than light; fact will fight with fact, case with case, reason with reason.
2. Of these two charges I see the creator, I see the source, I see the certain head and name.
3. But these kinds of excellences not only in our customs but even now in books are

scarcely discovered. Even the pages which used to contain that ancient severity have fallen into disuse.

4. Between the earth and heaven, in the same air, hang, separated by discrete intervals, seven stars which, from their movement we call planets. In the middle of these moves the sun, of the largest magnitude and power and not only the ruler of seasons and lands, but also of the stars themselves and of heaven. It is fitting for those judging its works to believe that this (the sun) is the spirit and mind of the entire world, this is the principal rule and spirit of nature. This one provides light and removes darkness, this conceals, this illuminates the remaining stars, this regulates from the use of nature the successions of the seasons and the year which is always being reborn; this scatters the gloom of heaven and even pacifies the clouds of the human mind; this one also lends his light to the other stars, extra bright, outstanding, looking upon all things, also hearing all things. . . .

5. 1. Do not shout!
2. Do not write a book!
3. Do not push the son!
4. Do not be pushed!
5. Do not destroy the city, oh soldiers!
6. Do not destroy the city, oh soldiers!
7. Destroy the city, oh soldiers!
8. Destroy the city, oh soldier!

6. 1. Hear, hear, senators, and learn the wounds of the republic.
2. Save therefore, judges, a citizen of good skills, of good parts, of good men.
3. Do not think that I today, when I respond to that man as just as he provoked me, have forgotten myself.
4. For which reason depart and remove this fear for me: if it is true, so that I may not be oppressed, but if false so that I may finally cease to fear.

7. 1. If only our sailors had conquered!
   optative
2. If only the sailors would conquer!
   optative
3. The sailors could conquer.
   potential

4. Should I walk to the sea?
   deliberative
5. Should we have walked to the sea?
   deliberative
6. Let us walk to the sea!
   hortatory
7. If only we had walked to the sea!
   optative
8. Should the soldiers not have walked to the sea?
   deliberative

8. 1. We have been born for honor and freedom; either let us have these things or let us die with dignity.
2. For who would not fear a god seeing and pondering and noticing all things and thinking that all things related to him, attentive and full of concern.
3. O the stupidity! Should I say stupidity or remarkable shamelessness?
4. Let some sport be given to the age, let youth be more free; let not all things be denied to pleasures; let that true and upright reason not always overcome; let desire and pleasure sometimes conquer reason.
5. If only I could discover true things as easily as refute false things!
6. If only you had never entered into an alliance with Caesar or had never pulled it apart!
7. For why should I have placed myself as an obstacle to your audacity?

9. 1. the poet singing
2. liberty destroyed
3. liberty destroyed by avarice
4. liberty destroyed by the avarice of the soldiers
5. the poet about to shout
6. the poet on the mountain about to shout
7. the poet on the mountain about to shout about liberty
8. the poet on the mountain about to shout about liberty destroyed by the avarice of the soldiers
9. The poet on the mountain who is about to shout about liberty which was destroyed by the avarice of the soldiers is dying.

10. The poet on the mountain who was about to shout about liberty which had been destroyed by the avarice of the soldiers died.
11. The boy walking to the sea fears the captured slaves.
12. The boy walking to the sea fears the slaves who were captured by the sailors.
13. The boy walking to the sea sees the slaves killing the animals.
14. The boy walking to the sea saw the animals which had been killed by the slaves.

10. 1. The queen whom the king fears is loved by the poet.
    acc. direct obj.
2. The king by whom the queen is feared hates the poet.
    abl. personal agent
3. The king whom the queen hates fears animals with large horns.
    acc. direct obj.
4. The animals which had been led to city by the king who hates poets were feared much.
    nom. subject
5. The animals who had large horns were killed by the soldiers of the king.
    dat. of the possessor
6. The bodies of the animals whose horns had been sold were being placed in the fire.
    possessive gen.

Chapter 9

1. 1. Because the slaves were extremely wretched, the king was giving gold to the people.
2. The king was giving gold to the people (supposedly) because the slaves were extremely wretched.
3. Although the slaves are most wretched, the king will not give gold to the people.
4. Since the king had given gold to the people, the slaves were not shouting.
5. When the king gave gold to the people, they shouted.
6. Because the queen had been captured, the king was preparing war.
7. The king was preparing war before the queen could be killed.

8. They were waging war until the king was killed.
9. They were waging war until the king should return.
10. Since the king had been killed, the queen was shouting.
11. Although the king had been killed, nevertheless the queen was happy.
12. When the moon departed, the light of day came.

2. 1. Then finally you will be killed, when no one so base, so desperate, so similar to you will be able to be found.
2. Nor for this reason are our speeches less effective because they arrive with pleasure to the ears of the judges.
3. For indeed what good man would not have been a creator of your death since the health and life of every excellent man rested upon it, the liberty and dignity of the Roman people (rested upon it).
4. But before I approach those things which have been disputed by you, I will say what I think about you yourself.
5. Since you speak about ancient things, make use of the ancient liberty from which we have degenerated even more than (we have degenerated) from eloquence.
6. Pompeius himself, incited by the enemies of Caesar and because he wished no one to be made equal with himself in respect to prestige, had completely turned himself away from his friendship.
7. But nevertheless men, although they are in violently disturbed circumstances, if at least they are men, sometimes are relaxed in their minds.

3. 1. The people fear that the avarice of the king will destroy the kingdom.
2. The poet was afraid that avarice had destroyed the kingdom.
3. The king deters the poets from writing books.
4. The king will not deter the soldiers from killing the poets.
5. The Romans did not doubt that empire was the greatest of goods.
6. The poet was begging the king that the books not be destroyed.

Answers to Exercises

7. The king will not destroy the books provided that the soldiers kill the poets.
8. The king wishes to kill the poets in order that the people may be free from books.
9. The poets were being killed by the king in such a way that the people feared much.
10. So great was the avarice of the king that the people now is a people of slaves.

4.
1. Was he so insane that he entrusted all his fortunes to the slaves of another person?
2. Let desire and pleasure sometimes conquer reason, provided that the following rule and control be maintained.
3. But now, in order that I may free myself from all ill will, I will put in the middle (i.e., explain) the thoughts of the philosophers concerning the nature of the gods.
4. But since, senators, something must be said by me on behalf of myself and many things (must be said) against Antonius, I ask one thing of you, that you listen to me in a friendly manner when speaking about myself, and another thing I myself shall bring about, that, when I speak against that man, you listen attentively.
5. You with that throat, with those flanks, with that gladiator's strength of your entire body, had drunk so much (of) wine at the wedding of Hippia that it was necessary for you on the following day to vomit in view of the Roman people.
6. Why were you either so friendly that you lent gold or so hostile that you feared poison?
7. Or were they afraid that so many men would be unable to overcome one man, strong men (would be unable to overcome) a weak man, swift men (would be unable to overcome) a terrified man?
8. Nor must it be doubted that there were poets before Homer.
9. For which reason depart and remove this fear for me; if it is true, in order that I may not be oppressed, but if false, in order that finally I may cease to fear.

5.
1. If the insane king destroys the kingdom, the poets will flee to Rome. (Future more vivid)
2. If the insane king had not destroyed the kingdom, the poets would not have fled to Rome. (Past contrary-to-fact)
3. If the son should not preserve his faith, the father would be most wretched. (Future less vivid)
4. If the son were not preserving his faith, the father would be most wretched. (Present contrary-to-fact)
5. If the son had not preserved his faith at that time, the father would now be most wretched. (Mixed contrary-to-fact)
6. If many poets walk in the city, they give peace to both the queen and the people. (Simple)
7. If the king should kill the poets, the people would fear. (Future less vivid)
8. If the insane king kills the poets, the people will fear much. (Future more vivid emphatic)
9. If the great poet had been killed by the insane king, the queen would have destroyed the peace. (Past contrary-to-fact)
10. If the great poet is killed by the king, the queen will destroy the peace. (Future more vivid)

6.
1. We would also have lost our memory itself with our voice if it were so much in our power to forget as (it is in our power) to keep silent.
2. Many jokes are customarily in letters which, if they should be exposed, would seem foolish.
3. If your parents feared you and you were not able to please them in any way (i.e., by any means) you would withdraw from their eyes (sight) to some other place.
4. But if some state were found in which no one sinned, a lawyer would be completely unnecessary among innocent men just as a doctor (would be) among healthy men.
5. But what would you say in opposition really if I should deny that I ever sent that letter to you?
6. The day would now run out if I should try to express the things which can be said against this thought.

7. 1. Poets came to the city in order that they might write books.
   2. So blind were the poets that they did not see the danger.
   3. There are people of the sort who love money more than liberty.
   4. The king because he loved money more than liberty was preparing war.
   5. The soldiers were seeking something of the sort which they would love more than money.

8. 1. What is there of the sort which you would not dare?
   2. Then finally you will be killed, when no one so foul, so desperate, so similar to you will be able to be found (no one) of the sort who would not say that it was done rightly. As long as there will be anyone of the sort who would dare to defend you, you will live.
   3. For what is there indeed, Catiline, of the sort which now in this city would be able to please you, in which there is no one, outside that conspiracy of desperate men, of the sort who would not fear you, no one who would not hate you?
   4. Decidius is sent with a few men in order that he may look over the nature of the place.
   5. Hear now, please, not those things of the sort which he did basely and intemperately against himself and his own private honor, but which he did impiously and monstrously against ourselves and our fortunes, that is, against the whole republic.
   6. For why should I have placed myself as an obstacle to your audacity (of the sort which) neither the authority of this body nor the opinion of the Roman people nor any laws were able to restrain?

9. 1. The king will give money to the poet when/if/because he sings.
   2. Although he was singing, nevertheless the king did not give money to the poet.
   3. The king would give money to the poet if he were singing.
   4. The king would not have given money to the poets if they had been captured by the soldiers.

5. If he would give money to the poets captured by the soldiers, the king would be loved by the queen.

10. 1. While the slaves were fleeing, the soldiers destroyed the city.
   2. When/if the slaves flee, the soldiers will destroy the city.
   3. If the slaves were fleeing, the soldiers would be destroying the city.
   4. When the city had been destroyed by the soldiers, the commander shouted that he was king.
   5. If the city had been destroyed by the soldiers, the commander would have shouted that he was king.
   6. If the city is destroyed by the soldiers, the commander will shout that he is king.
   7. While the commander was shouting that he was king, the slaves were fleeing from the city.
   8. If the commander is king, the slaves will fear much.
   9. If the commander had been king, the slaves would have feared much.
   10. Although the commander was shouting that he was king of the city, nevertheless the soldiers departed.

11. 1. And so when all of their fields had been destroyed, their villages and buildings had been burned, Caesar led the army back and settled it in winter camp.
   2. Although a small part of the summer remained, nevertheless Caesar hurried to set forth into Britain.
   3. And just as the old time saw what was the most extreme in liberty, so we (see) what in slavery, with even the exchange of speaking and listening having been removed through trials.

12. 1. We think that the queen is wretched.
   2. We think that the queen was wretched.
   3. We think that the queen will not speak to us.
   4. He thinks that the mothers of the dead soldiers are walking toward the sea.
   5. He thought that the mothers of the dead soldiers had walked to the sea.

Answers to Exercises

6. There is a rumor that the mothers of the dead soldiers will walk to the sea.
7. There was a rumor that the mothers of the dead soldiers would walk to the sea.
8. He says that the animals are being looked at by the boys.
9. He says that the animals were looked at by the boys.
10. He said that the animals were being looked at by the boys.
11. He said that the animals had been looked at by the boys.
12. He said that the boys would look at the animals.
13. He said that the animals would look at the boys.
14. No one believes that the king will kill the poets.
15. Who would believe that the king killed the poets?

13.
1. Is it believable then that so great a crime was committed for no reason?
2. Now you will understand that I am keeping watch for the safety of the republic much more sharply than you are for its destruction.
3. I was grieved, I was grieved, senators, that the republic which had formerly been saved by your counsels and mine would perish within a short time.
4. For there are and have been philosophers (of the sort) who believed that the gods have no concern for human matters. And if the opinion of these men is true, what devotion can there be, what sanctity, what religion?. . . However, there are other philosophers, and these indeed are great and noble, (of the sort) who believe that the entire world is managed and ruled by the mind and reason of the gods.
5. The clever man does not understand that he against whom he speaks is being praised by him, that those among whom he speaks are being criticized.

14.
1. We wonder why you are shouting.
2. We were wondering why you had shouted.
3. I do not know why they shouted.
4. Do you know to whom the king will give gold?

5. You knew to whom the king was going to give gold.
6. He did not wish to tell me how the soldiers had destroyed the city.
7. No one is able to tell me why the city is being destroyed by the soldiers.
8. Tell me by whom the king was killed.
9. He asked why we are not loved.
10. Who asked why we had not been loved?

15.
1. I (saw) what that man (was thinking and watching for) and that man on the other hand saw what I was thinking and watching for.
2. That man (saw) what I (was thinking and watching for) and I on the other hand saw what that man was thinking and watching for.
3. For what was the reason why Caelius wanted to give poison to that woman? But nevertheless it has not been said from where that poison came, how it was prepared.
4. And so today I will accomplish that he understand how great a favor he received from me at that time.
5. And just as the old time saw what was the most extreme in liberty, so we (see) what in slavery, with even the exchange of speaking and listening having been removed through trials.

16. If, judges, there should perhaps now be present someone ignorant of the laws, of trials, of our practice, he would undoubtedly wonder what is the great terribleness of this case because during holidays and public entertainments, when all law court business matters have been suspended, this one trial is being conducted, nor would he doubt that the defendant is being accused of so great a crime that, if this thing were neglected, the state could not stand.
1. Present subjunctive in the protasis of a future-less-vivid conditional sentence.
2. Present subjunctive in the apodosis of a future-less-vivid conditional sentence.
3. Present subjunctive in indirect question in primary sequence showing time simultaneous to the main verb.
4. Ablative of time when.
5. Ablative absolute.

6. Present subjunctive in a clause of doubting in primary sequence showing time simultaneous to the main verb.
7. Present subjunctive in a result clause in primary sequence.

17.
1. The king kills poets because they shout about liberty.
2. The queen says that the king kills poets because they shout about liberty.
3. The queen said that the king was killing the poets because they were shouting about liberty.
4. The queen says that the king killed the poets because they shouted about liberty.
5. The queen says the king will kill the poets because they shouted about liberty.
6. The queen was saying that the king had killed the poets because they were shouting about liberty.
7. The queen was saying that the king would kill the poets because they had shouted about liberty.
8. The queen was saying that the king who feared the people had killed the poets because they had shouted about liberty.
9. The queen was saying that the king who feared the people would kill the poets because they were shouting about liberty.

18. When the same man hears that there is a law which, in the case of rebellious and criminal citizens who have occupied the senate armed, who have inflicted violence upon magistrates, who have attacked the republic, orders a trial to be held daily, he would not disapprove of the law, he would ask the crime which is being handled in the trial; when he hears that no crime, no audacity, no violence is being called into trial but that a young man of outstanding talent, diligence, favor is being accused by the son of that man whom he himself is calling and has called, moreover that he is being attacked by the resources of a prostitute, he would not find fault with the loyalty of that man, he would think that the lust of a woman must be suppressed, he would judge that you are very hard working, for whom it is not permitted to be at leisure not even during the leisure that is common to all.
1. Subject accusative of an indirect statement.

2. Perfect subjunctive in a relative clause in indirect statement in primary sequence showing time prior to the main verb.
3. Ablative of description.
4. Present subjunctive in a relative clause in indirect statement in primary sequence showing time prior to the main verb

19.
1. He says that if war is waged in the province, the farmers flee. (Simple)
2. He says that if war is waged in the province, the farmers will flee. (Future)
3. He was saying that if war were waged in the province, the farmers would flee. (Future)
4. He says that if war were being waged in the province, the farmers would be fleeing. (Present contrary-to-fact)
5. He says that if war had been waged in the province, the farmers would have fled. (Past contrary-to-fact)
6. He was saying that if war had been waged in the province, the farmers would have fled. (Past contrary-to-fact)

20. And indeed, if you wish to pay attention diligently, (and) to judge truly concerning this entire case, you will so decide, judges, that neither would anyone for whom whether he wished (to do so or not) were permitted, have descended to this accusation, nor, when he had descended, would he have any hope (anything of hope), if he were not relying upon the intolerable lust and excessively bitter hatred of someone else.

The indirect question **utrum vellet** is the subject of **liceret**.

There is a subordinated conditional sentence that probably would have run as follows:

> Ad hanc accusationem non descendisset is cui licebat (dicere) utrum vellet (descendere an non), nec, cum descendisset, quicquam spei habuisset/haberet, nisi alicuius libidine et odio niteretur.—

21.
1. The queen thinks that the poets will be killed by the king.
2. The queen thought that the poets would be killed by the king.
3. The queen believes that on that day the citizens will fear the king.
4. The queen believed that on that day the citizens would fear the king.

Answers to Exercises

5. There was a rumor that the king would not be able to kill the poets whom the queen had hidden.

22. 1. That the king prepares war wearies the citizens.
2. It does not concern the poet whether the king destroys the books.
3. The poet said that all books would be destroyed.
4. The avarice of the king disgusts all.
5. It concerns all that liberty be preserved.
6. It wearies the queen to see the king.
7. It most greatly interests you to go away.
8. It will be necessary for all the citizens to read this book.
9. It will be necessary that this book be read by all the citizens.
10. It was not permitted for us that we live in peace.

23. 1. In such great happiness of the whole state was it necessary for me alone to be depressed?
2. Nevertheless it will not disgust (one) even with a rough and unfinished voice to have composed a record of prior slavery and a testimony of the present goods.
3. Neither did the soldiers embarrass me nor did you (embarrass) the leader.
4. When finally was it that what is permitted was not permitted?
5. For a long time already it was fitting for you to be led to death by order of the consul, Catilino; (it was fitting) for the destruction

which you devise against us to be brought against you.
6. What does it matter whether I wanted it to be done or that I am happy that it was done?

24. 1. Is it sweet to live?
2. I will go to the province in order to see the war.
3. I will go to the province in order to see the war.
4. I will go to the province for the sake of seeing the war.
5. To kill the poets was a terrible thing to do.
6. The poet wished to remain in the city.
7. The soldiers are afraid to destroy the city.
8. For the sake of destroying the liberty of all, the king wished to kill the poets.

25. 1. O an affair not only foul to see but even to hear!
2. Is it not therefore better to die a thousand times than to be unable to live in one's own state without the protection of armed men?
3. The day would now run out if I should try to express the things which can be said against this thought.
4. On behalf of my perpetual desire of maintaining and increasing your dignity, I ask and beg you, senators, that first, although it will be bitter to hear or incredible to have been said by Cicerō, you hear what I will say without offense, and that you not reject it before I have explained how it is.

INDEX